It is my sincer

this book would find within the pages healing

that only comes from our loving and caring

Abba-daddy!

I speak a blessing over your life that

you will come to know your Abba-daddy in

the full measure of his abiding mercy and

power that is available to his children.

Sincerely,

Your Sister and Your Father's Daughter,

Mission of the One Heart Series

To provide milk for the babe, and strong meat for the mature.
To rid all who come along on this journey of religious
traditions that make us white wash graves full of dead men's
bones! So, that we may say as the Apostle Paul: "OH" "That I
may know him, and the power of his resurrection, and the
fellowship of his sufferings, being made conformable unto his
death; if by any means I might attain unto the resurrection of
the dead. Not as though I had already attained, either were
already perfect: but I follow after, if that I may apprehend that
for which also I am apprehended of Christ Jesus. Brethren I
count not myself to have apprehended: but this one thing I do,
forgetting those things which are behind and reaching forth
unto those things which are before, I press toward the mark for
the prize of the high calling of God in Christ Jesus. Let us
therefore, as many as be perfect (pure in heart, italics mine), be
thus minded: and if any thing ye be otherwise minded, God
shall reveal even this unto you. Nevertheless, whereto we have
already attained, let us walk by the same rule, and let us mind
the same thing. Brethren, be followers together of me, and
mark them which walks so as ye have us for an ensample. (For
many walk, of which I have told you often, and now tell you
even weeping, that they are the enemies of the cross of Christ:
Whose end is destruction, whose God is their belly, and whose
glory is their shame, who mind earthly things.) For our
conversation is in heaven; from whence also we look for the
Saviour, the Lord Jesus Christ; Who shall change our vile
body, that it may be fashioned like unto his glorious body,
according to the working whereby he is able to even to subdue
all things unto himself. (Philippians 3:10-21, KJV)

Notice is hereby given that this author claims the full trade-mark rights to the all inferences of the "One", the "Heart", and the name "One Heart Series" utilized throughout the various books, tapes and any and all electronic media used to convey the One Heart Series Message.

Scripture quotations are from the KING JAMES VERSION of the Bible.
Printed in the United States of America

ISBN 0-9700976-0-3
LCCN 99-90785
With Oneness of Heart, An Inductive Study of Intimacy with God

---

ATTENTION ORGANIZATIONS, HEALING CENTERS, AND SCHOOLS OF SPIRITUAL DEVELOPMENT:

Quantity discounts are available on bulk purchases of this book for educational purposes. Special books or book excerpts can also be created to fit specific needs. For information, please contact Shekinah Publishing House, P.O. Box 156423, Fort Worth, Texas 76155, 1-877/538-1363.

She is a five-fold minister of the Gospel of Jesus Christ. Licensed in 1993 and Ordained in 1996, and serving her local church of The Potters House of Dallas, Texas. She is a Biblical Studies Instructor at The Potters Institute of Dallas, Texas and an author of a series of books on Inductive Bible Study.

The Series is called "One Heart" and cover how to be intimate with God. There are 5 books in this series. God has placed a strong teaching ministry within her spirit that speaks the truth in love, with a commandment to draw his people out and into an intimate relationship with their God.

God has wrought a mighty deliverance in her life from the baggage of physical, sexual, emotional, and religious bondage. Her testimony is that God is a mighty Deliverer and Restorer.

Patricia is available to share her testimony of deliverance and restoration to groups across the country and around the world. Contact her for

- Revival
- Lectures
- Biblical Seminars
- Writing & Publishing Seminars
- Mass Communication Workshops
- Keynote Address
- Family Seminars (Men, Women and Children)
- Ministry of Helps
- Transitional Housing Outreach

One "Echad" Heart International Ministries
Patricia E. Adams, President & Founder
Website: www.oneheartseries.com
Affiliate Program: www.oneheartseriesaffiliates.com
Radio Network: www.oneheartsoundmedianetwork.com
Email: author@oneheartseries.com

This book is dedicated to My Many Mothers -
Winnie
Rosie M.[1]
Marjorie
Tommie
Pinkie
Verma
Merlee
Rosie M.

It has taken many years to realize that because I did not have my biological mother that I was missing out. Recently, one of those that I was closest to and greatly impacted by went HOME and received her reward. And it was then that I realized that I was truly blessed and to be envied that God would bless me with so many mothers, but most of all that I have been influenced by all of them. Not all of them have been kind, but God! And I won't say which ones were mean and which ones were not. Today I know that what the enemy meant for evil, God took it and turned it into my good!

---

[1] It is not a typographical error. My first mother's last name began with an "M." and the last one mentioned her name too began with an "M."

ACKNOWLEDGMENTS

First and foremost I thank my "Lord and Savior" for the life experiences and revelation of the truth of His word concerning the trials that have tried me in the fire, and to the enemies of the light of the gospel of Jesus Christ! It is because of these fiery trials and those enemies that this work was accomplished.

To my son, without your understanding and support this work would not have been possible. It is a joy and pleasure being your mother. Much love to you my Precious!

And to God, who for many nights and early mornings called me into His presence and drew Rhema understanding of why so much pain and suffering had entered my life. He laid the solution before me, and asked me to apply it to the bitterness and pain of the aftershock of what had transpired in my life. For this there is no other that can take the place of Jesus Christ the Lover of My Soul!

We also wish to express special gratitude to the students who attended the initial Bible Study Training. Thank you for your faithfulness in drawing the Word of God out of my belly, and producing a river of living water within me. To Pastor Phillip P. Brown, Sr. and his Wife; Associate Pastor Ethel Brown, for their divine patience in allowing us to bring this material forth in a church bible study for 4 years.

A special appreciation to Pa-Pa and Mother Dear and Aunt Merlee for being there when needed the most. To Momma Tommie, Aunt Margie, Michele, Margie, and Junliah for coming alongside in their diverse ways.

Foundation Scripture:

"And the very God of peace sanctify you wholly; and I pray God your whole spirit and soul and body be preserved blameless unto the coming of our Lord Jesus Christ. Faithful is he that calleth you, who also will do it."

(I Thessalonians 5:23)

Now unto him that is able to keep you from falling, and to present you faultless before the presence of his glory with exceeding joy. To the only wise God our Saviour, be glory and majesty, dominion and power, both now and ever. Amen.

"What is man that though art mindful of him; the Bible records. Man is a tripartite being created in the image of God as an expression of God. The divine plan of God for his created man was that he would love Him with all of himself. This created being would have an absolute desire to fellowship with his creator; from an undivided heart.

Man was created to fulfill the purpose of God in the earth; that is to commune and glory in the benefits of God. The Word of God was the creative force that formed the heavens and the earth, and he alone holds the patent on his creation and the keys to the kingdom. Through the disobedience of one man, Adam; Satan gained legal access, permission to become the Prince of the Air, but not the Ruler of all the earth.

The Bible says that the earth is the Lords and the fullness thereof, and those that dwell within. Ownership has been Gods all alone!

A song was written that said "…What Satan said was his, has been ours all alone…"

Now, Saints Jesus Christ has completed the work that his father sent him to do, and nothing else is required or shall be done. It is finished! Therefore, we should not allow Satan to continue to deceive ourselves into giving away our authority.

If you do not give him access, he can not come in!

Jesus removed Satan's rights to entangle all areas of our lives through the plan of salvation, He restored us to our original posture in God. Yet, we perish because of a lack of knowledge of the provisions of salvation. Especially, when we protect the painful wounds and fearful memories of our lives from God's healing touch. We literally allow a legal playground to be built, played on, and ruled over by Satan and his imps.

When we receive the Holy Spirit into our hearts, he brings in the entire five-fold ministry tools to run a revival in our dead spirit. The Holy Spirit empowers us to operate as God had originally planned. He lifts us from the ashes of despair!

Ashes are used to speak figuratively in the Bible to express the total destruction of a captive city. Ashes are known to be easily scattered, perishable, and, therefore, worthless. For example, when Satan held us as sinners; we were his captive cities.

But when the Power of the Word, the Blood of Jesus and the Fire of the Holy Spirit destroyed, and stripped bare the stronghold, the threat, the penalty and the sting of sin – we were made free! When something is made it is customized to fit the owner. Those strongholds can no longer rule over us, unless we allow them to!

From that landmark of despair, God becomes our Master (Adonai), Owner and Lord. Symbolizing the authority of God and the covenant relationship from the beginning of creation until the ascension of Jesus Christ. Picture an organizational chart, and the Trinity is aligned across the Top; and in a connecting line the second row links and aligns with the first row. This is what the Trinity has done; it has included those who believe with the authority to sit in heavenly places. We are heirs, co-equals with the inheritance of Jesus. Remember the Bible records that, "The Lord said unto my Lord, "Sit thou at my right hand, until I make thine enemies thy footstool." (Psalms 110:1)

In Malachi 4:3, it says that to the Righteous, the wicked deeds of Satan are the "...ashes under the soles of our feet."

Table of Contents

CHAPTER 1
In the Beginning

WHICH WAY SHOULD I GO?

THE BIBLE SAYS THERE IS A WAY THAT SEEMETH RIGHT?

BUT THE END THEREOF IS DESTRUCTION!

FOLLOW ALONG AND LET US FOLLOW AFTER CHRIST!

THE STUDY OF ONENESS

1- In the Beginning

In the beginning, all of creation was gathered in one place, at the same time, on one accord; for the sole purpose of showing forth and expressing the glory of God. An absolute perfected praise was brooding and resounding out of the face of the deep with such crescendo and harmony under the direction of the original Maestro; our awesome God -- Elohim.

Elohim; the God of relationship was bonding with all of creation and all that he had created. God imparted the elements of relationship within all that He had created. Imparted with the ability to relate and be related to, and to reproduce that relationship in the Earth. The ability to reproduce can be found in the word "Zoe." It is the life force of God containing the sufficiency of God. God produced a show demonstrating His greatness at the theatre called the universe. He set the final act of the longest running play to be seen in the world; and entitled this act

"The Outward Expressions of God."

God imparted His life "Zoe," defined in the Hebrew language as to empower and quicken every living, moving, and breathing thing in and on the earth to perform according to His script. God blew His breath into a micro-organic clay vessel, and called it man, and he became a living soul.

At the fall this man became the first among the living dead! You see to obey God releases life and to disobey God releases death. Either way you are never the same!

It is impossible to be touched by God and not be changed forever!

God reminds us in His Holy Word that, it is in Him we live, move and have our being! Outside of Him we are the living dead! The breath, the (psuche) God breathed into the nostrils of this handiwork called man made him into a living soul, complete and lacking nothing. It is the very essence of God that hovered over and upon man and drew out of him the life of God. Drew him out to a fully equipped and co-existent man with the sole purpose of communing with an infinite God, and reproducing the image of God in the earth.

After all, "God said, let us make man in our image, after our likeness…" Adam's life was in God, and God was in Adam. When the life force of God touches us or things around us there is an outward sign.

Nothing God touches remains the same! Man (Adam) had no other choice, but to be quickened into a living soul. The Bible records this question, "What is man that thou art mindful of him?" Man is a spirit being made a little lower than the angels of heaven. He lives in a body made of dirt, and eats the dirt of the earth to maintain his physical house. His physical house will return to the dirt from whence it was taken, but his spirit will spend eternity in heaven or hell. The angels inquired of God, because of the way he cared for this being – I almost feel as if they were jealous when they asked God "Who is this man?" This man whose life is like a vapor, whose days are filled with troubles, and will one day have to vacate the earth and return to spend eternity in Heaven or Hell. Yes, God who is this man? A tripartite.

A tripartite, Webster defines is one being; divided into three parts; three-fold having three distinctive **corresponding** parts. God designed man with three distinctive parts to relate to a three part God-head.

What happened to our relationship with our maker, creator and friend?

God made us for Himself, and we have abused his creation! It does not matter if you backslide or side-slide, you are irrevocably a vessel marked and in need of your God! Even if you are physically, emotionally and spiritually bound and are trying to run away from God you will stand out as a marked man! Because he is married to the backslider. Let me testify a minute.

One night I went to a club while in a backslidden condition, and on this particular night I encountered someone that I had fellowshipped with in church before the presence of God. He was a preacher on the run, and I a preacher in denial. That night we found ourselves fellowshipping in one of Satan's churches in the presence of Satan! If you have ever been married to God, you should be identifying with me at this point. I can tell you that there existed at that moment in time for me what seemed to be a great big finger pointing to my soul and asking me what I was doing there?

We both sat and reminisced about the church services, and how the Lord had used us both, and we both had to admit that we knew we were out of place.

That night, in that club we both seemed compelled to admonish each other to make it back to the fold before it was too late, and before Christ returned. I praise God that the last report I had of this man of God; is that he was back in the fold, and of course so am I!

Thank God for his Grace and Mercy! I hope you come home real soon, maybe even today. He loves you just the way you are!

Because God never leaves us, nor forsakes us, it is we who leave God. Yet, God remains faithfully married to the backslider. Surely goodness and mercy shall follow us all the days of our lives! If we make our beds in hell, God follows after us desiring to show himself strong on our behalf. He is not lost, it is He who finds us, at the end of ourselves.

When you have been breathed on and marked by God for himself; you can't wash him off, you can't cover him up, and you surely can't hide from Him. Once the life of God gets in you, it gets on you and marks you with a mark that screams to everybody around you they belong to Me (God)! Thank God for that identifiable covenant mark; because it is a sure signal to Satan that he can only go so far. Just like God had a hedge of protection around Job, and even when the hedge was removed, God told Satan how far he could go.

The Word of God says that in Him we live, move and have our being. God is the life, and outside of God there is death. God was on the inside of Adam working on the outside of Adam, therefore there was nothing missing, and nothing broken in or with their relationship. There was SHALOM, meaning "wholeness" in Hebrew; no thing was broken or missing in this relationship. They experienced blessed wholeness on every level.

A wholeness that is both pluralistic and singular in nature as is revealed in Genesis 2:15-17, Genesis 3:16-17, and Genesis 2:25. The fulfilment of divine prophesy that a triune God would, did and still desires an intimate relationship with a tripartite man.

Jesus testified that he existed in the Trinity before the foundation of the world in John 10:30. He told His disciples that when they saw Him they also saw the Father, because He (Jesus) and the Father were one.

They were one in purpose yesterday, and they remain united in purpose today and forever more!

Upon further study of intimacy, I have found that we are being drawn into unity with God. The Hebrew word "Echad;" means tied together. In this tied together state there is not found a shadow or turning. Because our lives are hidden in Christ Jesus. There is no shadow (deception) in God the Father, God the Son or God the Holy Spirit. They exist with the exclusive mindset to do and say only what glorifies their loving purpose and plan for Gods' creation. They came post-fall to implement **the** way of escape; the plan of salvation. This plan existed before the foundation of the world that Jesus is that way of escape that led back to our Father, God.

Jesus snatched the total victory out of every temptation, trial or test we face in our lives.

When we receive the gift of salvation it is the planting of the seed of the tree of life in our born again spirit, and to come to it's full strength it must be watered with the Word of God!

So many believers, think that only Jesus could walk so perfectly! But we who were not perfect and who knew sin; have been made perfect and upright, and are now the righteousness of God through Christ Jesus. God looks at the heart while man looks at the outward appearance of men. It is my hope that you will continue this discourse with me and receive what I have received from our Father into my life. And that is "The Truth!" Because only this can set you free. Not some truth, or a piece of the truth or a truth, but the whole truth brings about liberty from bondage and sin that so easily makes us stumble.

I have heard from my youth that nobody could live a perfect life except Jesus, and that we are just lowly unworthy sinners. Well I can tell you that the damage that did to my soul and walk with God required the perfection of salvation to keep me from self-destructing. If it were not so, then I would not be sharing these words with you today! You see we go to the store and we buy ultra strength detergents, and ultra strength deodorants to handle those stubborn stains and odors.

But we fail to apply the simplicity of the word to our lives. "Ultra" is not new – it existed with God! If there is an "**ultra product** for our clothes and body;" Surely God is great enough to provide an ultra for our soul! God has an ultra and it is the "Blood of Jesus and the Word of God."

An ultra that will make you uncomfortable in the nasty ways of your past or present.

An ultra that will make you go straight when you want to go left.

An ultra that will make you leave somebody else's spouse alone and go home to your own, or wait for your own. **God has an ultra strength, and it is the "Word of God."**

In Hebrews 1:1-4 (Amplified Bible) it is found and reads as follows "In **many** separate revelations [each of which set forth a portion of the Truth] and in different ways God spoke of old to [our] forefathers in *and* by the prophets, [But] in the last of these days He has spoken to us in [the person of a] Son, Whom he appointed Heir and lawful Owner of all things, also by *and* through Whom He created the worlds *and* the reaches of space *and* the ages of time [He made, produced, built, operated, and arranged them in order]… …He is the sole expression the glory of God [the Light-being, the out-raying or radiance of the divine], and He is the perfect imprint *and* very image of [God's] nature, upholding *and* maintaining *and* guiding *and* propelling the universe by His mighty word of power. When He had by *offering Himself* accomplished *our* cleansing of sins *and* riddance of guilt, He sat down at the right hand of the divine Majesty on High, [Taking a place and rank by which] He Himself became as much superior to angels as the glorious Name (title) which He has inherited is different from *and* more excellent than theirs."

Now apply this to your life and you too will understand that we were once sinners and afar from God, but we have now been made righteous sons, daughters and joint-heirs with the one who was our way of escape; Jesus Christ and all of his anointing is available for the receiving of all those who would dare to believe on His Name!

There ought to be a difference in your understanding of who and whose you are at this point!

Since, the ultra has been applied to our lives, there remains a permanent sign that it has been applied! Just like when you use those ultra products the stain or odor is gone. Well! Well! God is forever reminded that the stain and odor of our sins has been removed; every time he looks at the blood of Jesus! Halleluia!!!!!!!!

Be Free, Be Free in the Name of Jesus! Be Loosed! Loosed from those old grave clothes and get out of that cemetery, already; and let the dead bury the dead!

Stop affirming your beliefs around just one scripture, and eat the whole book. The Church has used Romans 3:10 as a loophole in the Word of Gods' contract. It is sealed and irrevocable in the Blood of the Lamb. Whatever the saints of God have demonstrated in the earth before the world will be held to our account in the day of reckoning. The god of this world uses this to his advantage in the areas of our dilution and distortion of how faithful God is to those who call him.

The passage I have heard most is, Romans 3:10 says, "As it is written; There is none righteous, no, not one:" It is time to eat the whole loaf of manna! I have even heard this scripture preached as a paraphrase "Do as I say, not as I do, because I am not perfect, and I am only human."

No, rather let every man be a liar and God the truth!

His Word says we can do greater not lesser things than what Jesus performed during his earthly ministry. Presently Jesus' ministry is that of an advocate seated at the right hand of the Father as our mediator and way of escape for us from the temptations, trials and test of this life.

With God on our side we can go through the flood, the fire and the rain and not smell like mildew, smoke, and wet dogs. We have been empowered to be the righteousness of God, not lowly sinners saved by grace.

Perhaps you have heard this, been told this and even believe this. Don't tell me that you think you are still thinking that you are nothing more than a sinner saved by grace. Yes, Yes I know our righteousness is as filthy rags before God. But step back for a minute from tradition, and let's reason.

If God said that we are justified; seen by him as if we have never sinned.

And that we have become joint heirs with the perfect one Jesus Christ. And that the debt has been paid in full. Who are we to crawl around like dogs, when he says we are his sons and daughters.

I am not saying once saved always saved, obviously from the small amount of my testimony that I have shared in this text that can not be true. Because obviously I have been in a backslidden state; just like Hosea's wife Gomer.

Gomer represents the lukewarm spirit within the church, that prostitutes grace by straddling the fence between holiness or hell. One minute people can tell you belong to God, and the next minute not only do people question your salvation and so do you. I am speaking of believers whose hearts desires are to please God more than themselves, and who take the initiative to live in the resurrection power of God.

A sinner is one who **habitually** practices sin. A sinner **keeps on sinning the same sin or another without ever gaining dominion but being conquered.** Webster defined a sinner as one who sins, a reprobate a scamp. Is this how God sees us? No, I don't think so!

A Sinner practices the art of sinning! A Righteous man demonstrates rather than practice the grace of righteousness!

We have been made the righteousness of God through Christ Jesus.

In addition, when we worship we must worship Him in Spirit and in Truth.

John 9:31, says, "Now we know that God heareth not sinners; but if any man be a worshipper of God, and doeth his will, him he heareth."

So when God sees us the born again believer, he sees Jesus, and there is no fault in Him. Out of a perfected heart; one that is governed by and walks with the Holy Spirit. This type of heart desires to do righteousness and pursues the path of righteousness. God said to the believer that He writes the law on our hearts. Even in the Old Testament David confirmed that the patriarchs before the Resurrection could hide the Word of God in their hearts that they might not sin against God. It is now Post-Resurrection!

Since, we are presently able to access and appropriate the post-resurrection power of God through our born again spirit; this bold Holy Spirit does not possess the desire to sin or have a mind to sin. But the flesh of the old man is lead around by it's desires and lusts.

This is why we are to walk (agree with) the resurrected spirit of God so that we might not fulfill the lust of the flesh.

When we maintain a lifestyle and a mindset of sin, we are double-minded and unstabled. Therefore, we are tossed to and fro by every wind and doctrine. Jesus said a double-minded man should not expect to receive when he prays.

We must realize that because we have an advocate with the Father – seated interceding for us that we should repent quickly to remain "echad" tied up in God.

I remember the old saints singing a song that went something like this.

"I am wrapped up, tied up, and tangled up in Jesus, because He is my friend; he healed by body and told me to run on, he picked me up and told me to come on." That song reflects the difference between the committing of sin and being a sinner, they are not the same. A believer may commit a sin, but that does not make him a sinner. When the believer repents he is fully restored!

But a sinner will continue to sin the same sin over and over again with or without repenting. The sinner will make grace of no affect and crucify Christ afresh while being led by the desires of the flesh. But a child of God quickly turns back. Consider the prodigal son! When he turned and came to himself, he quickly returned to his Father's house and was restored to his former estate.

There is no record that he left again, because he came to himself and considered the pig sty no place for his Father's son.

II Peter 2:21-22 from the Message Translation makes this really plain, "If they've escaped from the slum of sin by experiencing our Master and Savior, Jesus Christ, and then slid back into that same old life again, they're worse than if they had never left. Better not to have started out on the straight road to God than to start out and then turn back, repudiating the experience and the holy command.

They prove the point of the proverbs, "A dog goes back to its own vomit," and, "A scrubbed-up pig heads for the mud."

Now if you still want to say you are a sinner, go ahead, but remember you will be sinning big time as a liar, and God says he hates a liar.

You choose!

God did not say that we would not be tempted, but He said that when we are tempted we do not have to yield to temptation.

Simply put; stop by, sit a spell, kick your shoes off, or make friends and entertain it.

The Lord lifts up the righteous. And the righteous are seated with Him in heavenly places. And the Lord is seated in the position of Intercessor for us in the time of trouble. And what belongs to Jesus, He upholds; recall Hebrews 1.

Now let us examine Romans 3:10. Firstly, there is a colon [:] after "one" in that passage of scripture, indicating a sequenced dialogue is following.

But before Romans 3:10, verse 9 opens up with two questions.

Then a response is given in verse 10 which acts as the introduction to this train of thought. Verse 10 ends with a semicolon [;] which in the earlier forms of English indicated that an important thought is following.

At the end of verse 10 there is a [:] colon which ties the thought back to verse 9, points forward to the end of Chapter 3. Although there are other sentences ending in periods throughout this discourse, it is the same and therefore, related.

Taking only one part of this passage is the same as taking only 1 days dosage of a 30-day prescription, highly ineffective.

Believers who want to remain babes will look for scriptures to justify and hide their failure to grow up in Christ. They will even say that nobody is perfect besides Jesus, I am only human, and I have needs.

Sinners are **governed and led** by their own human desires!

But the born-again believer is supernaturally empowered to overthrow the government of his own human desires. Because at his disposal is the power of God being poured into the natural. And it comes upon, from within our born again spirit onto the natural man enabling him/her to resist the temptation before them. Then the Holy Spirit comes alongside us and quickens; or rather thrust us into the presence of God, and enables a believer to do the will of the Father.

Christians' who experience difficulty with their walk oftentime will look for people who agree with their carnal thoughts and deeds. Someone who will affirm and give them quasi-permission [implied approval] that their lusts of the flesh must be given in to. And when the flesh is really wanting to have its way; the faltering christian will begin to make remarks; such as, 'they are not Jesus', and 'that he knows their hearts' -- and 'that they are only human'. And some will go so far as to say, surely, Jesus did not mean for us to live the same as he did, after all that was over 2000 years ago. Because Jesus did not have all of the stress and temptations, we have in our modern society! Wake up children of God!

Yes, Yes – sure he knows your heart, so you should stop pretending and putting on! Be true to yourself, you might as well because God already knows the truth about us. If you really are not ready and willing to overcome the temptation you will fall into sins snare. No matter how hard you pray, if you are hoping that God will look the other way this time while you go forward with the desires of your flesh, then you are deceiving yourself. Scripture says in Acts 17:30, that "And the times of this ignorance God winked at; but now commandeth all men every where to repent."

Because, there are too many of our sisters and brothers who are physically dying from their life-styles consequences of living in the wilderness of self-based living.

Choosing to live and die in the wilderness of self-based living. Never mind that Jesus has forever dealt a crippling blow to sins' power! Never mind that He has shed His blood! Never mind that He died once and for all! Never mind that He paid the bill we could not afford or desire to pay! Just keep on skipping along as if you have all the time in the world to get your act together. He said fear not because he has overcome the world.

God has given us the blueprint to the exit out of the

wilderness in His Word. Just like little children who throw temper tantrums, will stop when they are shown who is in control. So too will our flesh throw temper tantrums, and we need to check it and show it whose in control "God."

Whatever causes us to fall into sin; He has given us the way out. We are to discern the snares of the enemy up ahead and avoid the snares like we avoid a pit full of snakes. We are to be akin to the tribe of Issachar; which were renowned throughout the Christian community for their ability to discern the times and the seasons of God in their lives and the lives of God's people.

We are the chosen generation and royal preisthood that has been given GRACE.

God's ability on and in us to take us all the way through, our wilderness and valleys. Our wilderness is composed of ancestral and personal bad choices. Containing mazes, land mines and undetonated grenades – steer clear!

When we accept the gift of salvation from God the battle begins. The battle of the wilderness is between the old man and the righteous man. Satan does not let go until you show him the Blood and the Word is active in your life!

We are vessels containing the old spirt and the old soul, warring against the new man. Mark 1:9, illustrates this battle. "And it came to pass Jesus… was baptized…And straightway coming up out of the water…And immediately the Spirit driveth him into the wilderness. In addition, he was there in the wilderness forty days, tempted of Satan. The Angels of God ministered to Jesus in the midst of this great test, because of his obedience. When we obey God, all of heaven is attentive to us. I read this quote on a church billboard, "Integrity is what you do when nobody is watching."

The body is use to obeying the edicts of the old man, but the new man yearns earnestly after the things of God as a deer panteth after water. The new man as the Word of God strengthens him, he begins to reel in the old man and place him under the influence of God. The more you feed on the Word of God the stronger the new man becomes and the sooner and more completely you experience deliverance and victories in your walk.

You are no longer a divided house, and a city without walls, but a united front built on the rock of ages. That old mans nature has to be tamed and informed that the love you once had for it, is gone and it will no longer rule your life!

Satan was there in the wilderness the entire 40 years of the children of Israel's journey and he will be there with you in your wilderness, but you have a way of escape. Every place in the Old Testament where the children of God were overtaken, Jesus walked through those places and led captivity captive.

The children of Israel embarked on a journey to the Promised Land that was suppose to take 40 days. The wilderness is symbolic of the old mans wild and rebellious nature. Satan will tempt us in the wilderness of the old man.

That is why we are admonished to walk in the Spirit and the not after the flesh, so that we may become trees planted by the rivers of living waters. Don't close the book yet!

Satan was there in the wilderness the entire 40 years with the children of Israel, as they journeyed. They had a way of escape, but refused it – and many died without experiencing all God had for them. He will be there with you in your wilderness too, but you too have a way of escape, and the power to come out.

Every place in the Old Testament where the children of God faltered and were overtaken, Jesus walked through those same places and led captivity captive. There lies the key to your permanent deliverance from the perpetual, seemingly unyielding mountain. It will work if you work it! The children of Israel embarked on a journey to the Promised Land that was only to take 40 days. The wilderness is symbolic of the old mans wild and rebellious nature. Satan uses the old man to tempt us the in the wilderness and causes us to set ourselves up, mishandle and abuse ourselves.

Satan is the originator, the Father of Child Abuse! He uses and abuses his children. He lures them with things they desire and then attempt to destroy them with the fulfillment of that desire. He takes us up to the mountain, like he did Jesus and tells us to pick what we want and worry about the consequences later. When we choose what we feel we can not do without at all cost, Satan takes that and causes it to tarnish and imprison us. No one would fall for his tricks if he offered things that did not appeal to us. And the disturbing thing is that it is ours already, but Satan wants us to chose his way of getting it over God's way.

That is why we are admonished to walk in the Spirit and the not after the flesh, so that we may become trees planted by the rivers of living waters. Don't close the book yet!

Remember for every level you reach there is a greater attack by the Devil and his imps. But God has a greater anointing for every level. Jesus was anointed for every level of his ministry. The many levels of Jesus' anointing enabled him to do the many miracles throughout the Gospels.

When Jesus was preparing to confront death, hell and the grave he received the anointing to die and be resurrected. Because he was willing and obedient to do all his Father commanded. What Jesus received in the Garden of Gethsemane carried him through the Crucifixion, Death, Hell, Grave, Resurrection and Ascension. Remember he laid down his life it was not taken. Even though we have been taught that he was killed. You can not kill someone who gives away his life. Thus he was able to take it back up again at the appointed time.

He was only asleep – abiding alone in the ground, he became a crushed seed that released the faith to reproduce the divine nature after its' kind.

Remember the story of the talents they reproduced after their kind. Use what you have and you will receive double. Jesus' anointing doubled each time the virtue went out of him, and each time he overcame the temptations before him. Because he used what God had given him and each time he received an increase.

Matthew 26:39 says, "And he went a little farther, and fell on his face, and prayed, saying O my Father, if it be possible, let this cup pass from me: nevertheless not as I will, but as thou wilt."

It was at that moment that Jesus denied himself, and received the anointing to lay down his life and pick it up again. He triumphed over the flesh permanently when he surrendered his will to God's will. Which is another checkmate against the five, I wills of Satan found in Isaiah. Jesus did what the first Adam could not do, deny himself.

The believer has been given access to his power and empowered to do the same. For every wall of separation that existed; Jesus became the doorway through the wall. What are you tempted with today, it doesn't matter Jesus is the door through it! You have to become righteousness minded, and as you do you will become less sin minded. Don't focus on the old man, but focus on the new man!

If you will refuse to feed that sin nature what it really wants, and feed it the Word of God. Just as a baby is given only what it is able to digest, not the whole of it. But the part of the Word that sparks life in that dead area of your life. Scripture records that when Jesus told Peter that the knowledge he had expressed that Jesus was the Son of God; would be the knowledge that Jesus would build His church upon, and that the gates of Hell would not prevail against it.

What God gives you is rhema, that you turn into knowledge as you use it. As you use that knowledge God builds on it before you know it what use to be a weakness becomes a strength.

Well that one scripture that speaks to you the most when you are being tempted is that rhema that God is giving you at that very moment using it turns into knowledge that will cause you to be built up, and the gates of hell unable to prevail against you. At another time it may be a different scripture; but one day it will be the whole Bible! Because your confidence will be in the one who spoke the words and not the words alone.

John 3:29-32, 36 in the Amplified Bible says that "He who has the bride is the bridegroom; but the groomsman who stands by and listens to him rejoices greatly *and* heartily on account of the bridegroom's voice. This then is my pleasure and my joy, and it is now complete. He must increase, but I must decrease. [He must grow more prominent; I must grow less so] He who comes from above (heaven) is [far] above all [others]; he who comes from the earth belongs to the earth, and talks the language of earth [his words are from an earthly standpoint]. He Who comes from heaven is [far] above all others [far superior to all others in prominence and in excellence]. It is to what He has [actually] seen and heard that He bears testimony, and yet no one accepts His testimony [no one receives his evidence as true]....And he who believes in (has faith in, clings to, relies on) the Son has (now possesses) eternal life.

...But whoever disobeys (is unbelieving toward, refuses to trust in, disregards, is not subject to) the Son will never see (experience) life, but [instead] the wrath of God abides on him [God's displeasures remains on him; His indignation hangs over him continually]."

We are now heirs and joint heirs through Christ Jesus! What has you separated from God, or rather who hinders you that you do not run?

At the point where Jesus prayed for his persecutors, and just like Job when he prayed for his friends. When the Bible tells us to pray for those who despitefully use us; it is for the good of our generations now and later.

We must not allow anything to keep us from being fruitful and multiplying, subduing and having dominion!

When Jesus prayed for his enemies, commended his spirit, and gave up the ghost he received the anointing to multiply. He became the first begotten from the dead, and we as believers are the mutliplied dead from Ezekiels visions. When we accept salvation we go through the death, burial and resurrection.

We who were once dead in trespasses were prophesied to by Jesus as Ezekiel did in the Valley of Dry Bones.

We were prophesied to so that our dry bones might live, and live more abundantly.

Jesus was the first begotten of the dead, when he arose, he multiplied, just as a seed that is planted in the soil will multiply at its appointed season. So when Jesus the seed of righteousness was planted in the earth it was imputed to the sleeping righteous and they were empowered to get up! A seed bore after its' kind, righteousness begat righteousness, and the righteous were seen in the city! Don't you see this is why you are the righteousness of God through Christ Jesus! When Jesus got up, you and I got up too! We got up as one!

One with the Father, one with the Son, and one with the Holy Spirit; therefore in total oneness!

PRAISE GOD! I felt a release in your understanding. I declare that the Spirit of the Living God is falling fresh on my sisters and brothers at this very moment, plucking the scales from their eyes so they may know Jesus in the power of HIS resurrection. In Jesus Name Amen!

Now look as far as your eyes can see in the spirit, and take the new ground you have gained looking ahead to the author and finisher of our faith. Press ahead, and forget those things that are behind, and reach toward the prize of a higher calling in Christ Jesus.

The sooner you fall out with your past, the sooner you can get up out of your self-created wilderness.

You can stop crying and moaning toward Heaven and asking God, why so much pain?

I know, breaking up is hard to do when you want to hold on to the familiar. But when you are fed up with the turmoil and fallout of the poor decisions you and your parents made – you will cry ABBA FATHER and receive the spirit of adoption and no longer live as bastards! We are not fatherless!

We have to make a break with the old man to get to the other side of the Jordan, we have to fall out with the familiar on this side of the Jordan. The Jordan River is biblically known as a place of decision making. Are you making a decision, have you made a decision to press your way out of the wilderness!!! The song of salvation that poured from the lips of Miriam and the women of Israel as they crossed through the Red Sea, and it is still being sung today for us in Heaven.

The children of Israel refused to fall out of agreement with the familiar places (Egypt), and died on the Egyptian side of the Jordan. We have too many believers who have been saved for decades and still wrestle and die on the same side of the Jordan in the wilderness.

Those who chose to be on the Lord's side crossed over to the Canaan side of the Jordan.

There is a saying, you can take them out of Egypt, but you can't take Egypt out of them; or you can lead a horse to water but you can't make the horse drink. Can people tell whether you are a saint or a sinner?

Romans 3:9-31 draws a parallel between the sinner and the saint. It says, "What then? are we better than they? No, in no wise: for we have before proved both Jews and Gentiles, that they are all under sin; As it is written, There is none righteous, no not one: There is none that understandeth, there is none that seeketh after God. They are all gone out of the way, they are together become unprofitable; there is none that doeth good, no, not one.

Their throat is an open sepulchre; with their tongues they have used deceit; the poison of asps is under their lips: Whose mouth is full of cursing and bitterness: Their feet are swift to shed blood:...

Destruction and misery are in their ways: And the way of peace have they not known: There is no fear of God before their eyes. Now we know that what things soever the law saith, it saith to them who are under the law: that every mouth may be stopped, and all the world may become guilty before God....by the deeds of the law there shall no flesh be justified in his sight: for by the law is the knowledge of sin..."

Then the dialogue changes to speak of the righteous beginning with verse 21.

We are now switching to those who have received the righteousness of God through his son Jesus Christ "...But now the righteousness of God which is by faith of Jesus Christ unto all and upon all of them that believe: for there is no difference: For all have sinned, and come short of the glory of God;...

Being justified (restored as if you never sinned (mine)) freely by his grace through the redemption that is in Christ Jesus: Whom God hath set forth to be a propitiation through faith in his blood, to declare his righteousness for the remission of sins that are past, through the forbearance of God; To declare, I say, at this time his righteousness: that he might be just, and the justifier of him which believeth in Jesus…

Where is the boasting then? It is excluded. By what law? of works? Nay: but by the law of faith. Therefore we conclude that a man is justified (given a new identity (mine) by faith without the deeds of the law. Is he the God of the Jews only? is he not also of the Gentiles? Yes, of the Gentiles also: Seeing it is one God, which shall justify the circumcision of faith, and uncircumcision through faith. Do we then make void the law through faith?

God forbid: yea, we establish (carry out, fulfill inwardly – until there is an outward expression of (mine)) the law."

Children of the Most High God, the sinner is waiting on you and I, to decide that yes, God did mean that we are righteous! And those who come to Him, have their lives hidden in Christ Jesus! Why receive salvation if I still get called by the title that identifies me with Satan! Christ has changed our names and we are saints and children of the Most High God – El Elyon!

It is with this purpose and intent in mind from my heart that I write this as God has revealed himself as Jehovah M'Kaddesh in my life – the one who sees, sanctifies and justifies me through Christ Jesus. I too had to fall out with myself to see his glory in the land of the living! Without God we can do nothing. But with God all things are possible unto those that (who) means you right there reading this book) believe.

Somebody shout YES, I am a believer. Have you, or will you stand at the altar of your heart and declare to God that you want Him to come and live within, so that you can be like Him.

So you can walk out your destiny before six (6) people carry you to a garden, where the only thing that shows you were ever on this planet is a flowery tombstone.

God has sent his son Christ Jesus as a sign of what was, shall be and is to come. But in the meantime we have "GREATER WORKS" to do. So, once again in the beginning they were on one accord until the fall, and the great work that Adam had done was temporarily interrupted. Man could no longer come directly to God after the fall, a mediator was the line of communication to heaven, and even he was subject to death if his hands were unclean.

Can you imagine having to wake one morning with a desire to talk to God, and being confronted with silence – and waiting on another man to sanctify himself before taking your request to God.

The fellowship between God and his creation was broken by the fall, therefore man became self-centered instead of God-centered. We have a High Priest once and for all today! His name is Jesus!

Jesus became our sacrifice, ransom and mediator, drawing us back to God. To a place of restoration and empowerment to walk in oneness of heart as God had done before. Genesis says that God walked with Adam and Eve in the cool of the day. Jesus is pouring out his spirit as our comforter, paraclete, and enabler; our assistant that sticks closer than a brother. He gives us strength for our inabilities; essentially his personality.

What is the personality of that ONE who has come? What is he like? The perfected Christ who transforms us into overcomers.

Let's examine the word transform, and the prefix trans. I stumbled on this particular word, and even though you may not understand why I included, just bear with me for a moment. The word is "transpone" meaning situated on the farther side of a bridge. Now the prefix trans, means across, allowing for a reciprocal perspective.

Let's go back to the word "transpontine" for a moment, "pont" is from the Latin meaning bridge. So if I were to make the following sentence; "Jesus is my transpontine."

Would you gather by now that I am saying that He is our bridge, across troubled waters. Well this is what I am saying, he is the bridge that allows us to cross over to the Canaan side of the Jordan river. Now let's look at the word "transform." Remember the prefix "trans" means across.

"Form" means to change the form or outward appearance of, to change the condition, nature, or function of; convert, to change the personality or character of, suggests a change in basic nature that seems almost miraculous. (Miriam-Webster, 1988 by Simon & Schuster, Inc.)

Joshua 5:6, "For the Israelites walked forty years in the wilderness till all who were men of war who came out of Egypt perished, because they did not hearken to the voice of the Lord; to them the Lord swore that He would not let them see the land which the Lord swore to their fathers to give us, a land flowing with milk and honey. So it was their uncircumcised children whom He raised up in their stead…And the Lord said to Joshua, This day have I rolled away the reproach (*shame, mine*) from you."

So when we were sinners we were transformed; carried across to the other side, and circumcised. The other side being the opposite of where we were "sinners" and transformed into righteousness; by God through Christ.

Jesus is the bridge and mediator of a new and excellent covenant; the fulfillment of the Old Testament and the manifestation of the New Testament.

Jesus has placed his Word in our hidden man the 'Holy Spirit" and written it upon the tables of our hearts and when the two are reconciled during our worship of Him in Spirit and in Truth we are well able to be overcomers in the Earth.

We can now go from glory to glory, and faith to faith, not from sin to sin as believers. To get somewhere you have to leave where you are, don't you? So whose on the Lord's side? And how do we stay on the Lord's side?

By following the leading of the Trinity and the Holy Spirit. He is the resurrected and ascended spirit of Jesus being poured out into earthen vessels. Since, Jesus was and is 'one' with his Father, we are receiving the Father too!

The Holy Spirit is the eternal flame and spirit of the Word of God that was made flesh in Jesus. When Jesus was crushed like the olives were crushed to obtain oil for the temple, while he was in the Garden of Gethsemane, he was being prepared as our fuel to light our tabernacle. Now we have this treasure being poured out and into our earthen vessels freely and legally.

Therefore, you and I are not of this world, we are just passing through in this strange land on our way to our homeland. We carry in us; as born again believers the spirit of the Father and the Son, being expressed through the Holy Spirit. We are the salt that brings purification to those we witness to and a lamp showing those we encounter the way of salvation. We are living epistles and testifiers of his goodness and mercy!

We are the illuminators of darkness. The light of the Word. The lamp to their feet, and the Spirit of the Word that cuts the thorns, and briars from their hearts. Preparing a way of the Lord, leading them out of the wilderness.

When we walk in a room where there is darkness it ought to lighten up. The Holy Spirit quickens our fleshly mortal body and enables us to do great exploits equal to the amount of Gods' word we have consumed in our spirit, it is like the fire of the burning bush, brilliantly on fire but not consumed by the fire. Little Word, little Exploits!

Little Word, little fire! If it is worth doing, it is worth doing all the way! We must move from being luke-warm because it is the playground of Satan!

Some of God's people have been closet associates with the Anti-Christ. What did she say! Stop, hold up -- I know you are about ready to put this book down, but hold on and let us reason together. The scripture says that if He/Christ is for us He is more than the world against us, and we are either for him or against him. To be "one", is an outward expression of the in working of the gift of salvation through the Holy Spirit in our hearts.

Allowing access to our hidden hurts by the only one whom really knows us, and that is God. He comes in to make our hearts whole.

When we are not whole-heartedly serving Him we are displeasing to the call and election on our lives as a believer. Can you think of ways you have partnered with the Anti-

Christ (Satan)? Believers look up for your redemption draweth nigh.

If we follow the flesh, we can not fulfill the things of the Spirit. The prefix 'anti-' in any dictionary means against and it should not take a greater explanation than this to open our eyes. God said that he; the Spirit of Truth would open the blinded eyes.

So, in the name of Jesus, child of God, I command the scales of deception to disengage from the eyes of your understanding. May you arise and the enemies of God be scattered from you right now! Amen.

How, is it possible for a Christian to be against Christ? A carnal, unregenerate, immature Christian can be against Christ. When a believer refuses to walk in the light, as God is in the light. He is open territory for the works of the flesh. Walking continuously in the light allows us to see our true selves.

Loyalties to traditions handed down by great and grand ancestors to our generation of religious and familial traditions and customs have kept many of us in bondage.

I have come to know that if the customs and traditions that I practice and hand down to my generation are not God centered, then there is room for unwitting bondage in my household. Especially in the areas of man-made traditions and customs. We have spent so much time achieving and pursuing outward acclaim and fame that we have lost focus on the ultimate acclaim; which is the kingdom of God. We possess all of the trappings of religion outwardly, having a form of godliness without the possession of the power of God on the inside.

We have become comfortable and complacent in our traditions and customs; and made them ours in spite of the calling of God that often requires that we walk a path less traveled.

Well God is not coming back for your granddaddy and mommies' denomination, customs or traditions, but for His glorious and overcoming church!

Why do we attend or linger in the ruts of the same old path around the mountain of the wilderness. Trudging along, hoping we will get to the promised land, and blaming the leadership when we don't make any progress in our Christian walk. Even roaches move forward! We dig gardens and recycle soil and examine roots of plants and trees; but we fail to examine our own roots. We buy all types of plant foods, supplements and miracle formulas to improve our plants rate of survival and growth. We will even destroy a crop if it falters, but we will continue in the same path year after year and see no progress in our spiritual lives, but yet we choose to remain out of tradition.

Maybe you want to die in the wilderness of life; but not I.

I recall when I was on the club scene, if the place was not "jumping" when I got there and I could not get it jumping, I had no other choice but to go and find someplace else to go. I was determined not to spend my money, my time or my energy in a dead atmosphere.

So why do we go to church where we can fall asleep, sit in the same pews or find another miserable person to get hooked up with. Church was not designed by God to be a social club; but a place of refuge for the wounded to be healed. How long has it been since you have had a healing in your spirit, soul, mind or body.

I refuse to be bound by customs and traditions, and fear of breaking with the familiar in any area of my life. I pray that you too will listen to the voice of God and allow him to lead you where you need to be.

The place of "be" includes; family, friends, church, job and marriage. Some relationships are just pure "toxic"; meaning that if everytime you are exposed to the people, places or things you leave with a dagger sticking in your heart the size of a railroad spike – you need to make some changes. The Bible commands us to lay aside every weight and every sin that so easily besets us (sidelined) in the book of Hebrews.

The wisest man in the Bible was Solomon, and he wrote in Ecclesiastes that, there is a time and a season for everything under the sun.

Throughout the Bible there was a time and a season to go and come, and be still. Why would you think God would desire for you to become stagnant in any area of your life?

When he gave his only begotten Son to break the bands of bondage off of you; so that you might have a right to the tree of life, and life more abundantly!

If you want the things of God you have got to fall out with the old man, the familiar things and do the unfamiliar things and go to the unfamiliar places he leads you to!

Abram did it; he left his Father and his homeland and went in search of all God had for him. He cut a blood covenant with God in his flesh through circumcision, and received an exceeding great reward for letting go of the most sensitive part of flesh on a man's body. It was this ultimate act of obedience that caused God to change his name.

You see flesh is ultra-sensitive, and easily offended, but Abram was willing to let go of those things that offended him and made him insensitive to God. The foreskin of the male genital has to be handled with care and cleaned religiously to avoid infections, and can't stand too much pressure. But, to get to the plan of God, the force of the hammer of God, which is the Word; has to be applied to the sensitive areas of your fleshly heart. Abram's willingness to sacrifice the area of his body that required the most time to care for to become one with God was pleasing to God.

Because of Abrams' obedience, he received a new name and commanded blessings from the hand of God. A name, Abraham "that meant Father of Nations."

God will not tarry or strive with man or the church forever. He will accomplish his will with or without our help. It is a more desirable place to be found standing on the Lord's side when He returns; than against the Messiah and His Anointing. Do not continue to allow filthy habits and religious doctrines to be exalted above the reality of the Word of God in your life.

So we must cease to be sinners, and become the salt and light that preserves his Word until his coming, and shines the light in the darkness for those who are looking for the Messiah. He has commanded us to occupy until he comes, how are you occupying?

People shall know that we are his disciple's; ones who have been trained by the master to do as the master has instructed. Those are known by their love one for another, loving your neighbor and your enemies. If you have ever been wounded then this must seem like a monumental task to you. Do not be deceived God is not mocked, whatever a man sows that he shall reap.

God is not deaf or blind that he does not see! But who are you to stand against Him.

I speak as one who has forgiven much by faith, and not by how I felt! Forgiveness is not a feeling but an act of faith. Simply you forgive with tears in your eyes and pain in your heart, and a frog in your throat!

You do this, and he will deal with the perpetrator, the pain, the frog, and the tears, in his own way and his own time!

Since you were once deserving of death, who are you to stand against the role of God as Savior and Avenger in someone else's life.

Just because someone doesn't or did not love you the way that you think they should or could have, doesn't mean they did not or don't love you with all they had or have.

We all know someone, or have known someone or persons who have not loved us as we hoped they would. Whether they were biological, or intimate, or you were victimized by both. They only gave you what they had, but now it is time to move past what they did not have to give us and give ourselves what we deserve!

Freedom from carrying around the dead weight of the people who have left us feeling empty and neglected and move into position to receive.

When a hand is closed it can not receive. When a heart is closed and cluttered with dead issues there is no room for agape love or any type of love to flow. We can only be loved at the capacity we have made available.

Spring is in the air friends, in the natural and the spirit, while we spring clean our houses, garages and offices, how about the clutter in our souls.

Just by faith, not by feeling, release those who have hurt you in the past and the present from a debt they can not pay, the check you are waiting to cash will bounce anyway, because remember they can not give you what they don't have.

Be free in the marvelous name of the lover of your soul Jesus Christ!

When we harbor hatred, malice, envy, jealousy, and all the other works of the flesh in our heart then we are in darkness as those who have not comprehended the light, according to John 1:5. As people who walk in darkness and fulfill the things of the dark are not sons, but bastards. And all darkness has been placed under Jesus' feet, according to Psalms 18:9. So where does that place us when we dwell in darkness.

Are you residing in this position of dishonor? This is not the position he ordained for you and I, is it? We are to be above and not beneath, royal priest, but unless we quit deceiving ourselves there is a place reserved for the deceived and the deceiver and its called Hell.

If you are still with me, and will stay with me through the end of this book, I am believing God for shackles to fall off. I am placing myself in agreement with you and believing God that this revelation will rise up in your belly and overthrow the dark recesses of your spirit, soul and mind.

Arise and come hither to my Fathers' house with me as we consider the conclusion of the whole matter.

Genesis 1:31, says "And God saw every thing that he had made, and, behold it was very good." Goodness, exists in the continual unity of communion with God.

You have a choice to make! And that is life or death, blessing or cursing!

Remember you have a free will. If you did not have a free will then God would be a Dictator and not the true God who gave you a choice to serve him! Genesis 3 records the thoughtfulness of a loving God and Lord giving his creation a "free will." Without a free will man would have never experienced visualy, intellectually, emotionally, physically, auditorily and tastefully the provisions of God around him. You would have been relegated to what he desired only. Remember, he said that he would give us the desires of our heart. What Dictator do you know or have read about in history who has given you that opportunity?

What if God had given man a lobotomy; a partial removal of his brain as his punishment for surrendering the deed of the Earth over to Satan? Allowing man to have only the part of the brain that would allow us to serve him; we would be on auto-pilot or pre-conditioned to do and say only what God allowed. But God left man with the ability to pursue his hearts desires, no matter how depraved.

To have done otherwise, would have made him like man, and not God. Men try to control through supreme rule and authority over other men; but God pursues us as like the loving and forgiving Father towards the prodigal son.

It took the eyes, mind, thought and sensibility of God to enable man to see a thing with a long trunk and call it an elephant before it could become an elephant and begin to act like an elephant. God has not set his love upon us for naught, but that we might come to Him with a sincere and repentant heart and taste and see that He is good and loving!

He still wants us to have dominion and subdue the earth, and not each other. He gave us the ability to take in the fulness of the entire picture.

In the book of Genesis God showed forth his personality "Elohim" the God of relationships in the creation of the entire universe.

God created, called, blessed, said, moved, divided, set, ended, rested, sanctified, planted, took, commanded, formed, caused, saw and made the Earth and they that dwell therein.

The power of the personality of God in the expression of Elohim in the Garden was God relating to and through all he had done.

The Creative God of every relationship. An inherent relationship between God and man was in that name.

An elephant will not procreate with a rhinoceros, because they do not identify with each other, they know their own. Recall, God's man was made in his likeness, and the heavens and the earth made to declare his glory. Romans 8:22 says that the whole creation groans for his return.

God gave man a soul that would always look upward for dialogue with the one whom he identified and related to. After the fall, man related to himself rather than to God. The birth of every root of sin is recorded in the book of Genesis. Self-pleasers do not seek or desire to please God, which makes them idolaters. A self-pleaser sets themselves above God as the object and center of attention. What areas have you set up above God?

Nothing was to hold mans' attention span like that but God. Man lost his sense of God. His relationship had been three-fold before the fall, and to restore man back to God would require a three-fold restoration.

In I Peter 1:2-9 of the the Amplified Bible it reads "Who were chosen *and* foreknown by God the Father and consecrated (sanctified, made holy) by the Spirit to be obedient to Jesus Christ (the Messiah) and to be sprinkled with [His] blood: May grace (spiritual blessing) and peace be given you in increasing abundance [that spiritual peace to be realized in and through Christ, freedom from fears, agitating passions, and moral conflicts]…

…Praised (honored, blessed) be the God and Father of our Lord Jesus Christ (the Messiah)! By his boundless mercy we have been born again to an ever-living hope through the resurrection of Jesus Christ from the dead, [Born anew] into an inheritance which is beyond the reach of change *and* decay [imperishable], unsullied and unfading, reserved in heaven for you, Who are being guarded (garrisoned) by God's power through [your] faith [till you fully inherit that final] salvation that is ready to be revealed [for you] in the last time……[You should] be exceedingly glad on this account, though now for a little while you may be distressed by trials *and* suffer temptations, So that [the genuiness] of your faith may be tested, [your faith] which is infinitely more precious than the perishable gold which is tested *and* purified by fire.…[This proving of your faith is intended] to redound to [your] praise and glory and honor when Jesus Christ (the Messiah, the Anointed One) is revealed. Without having seen Him, you love Him; though you do not [even] now see Him, you believe in Him and exult *and* thrill with inexpressible and glorious (triumphant, heavenly) joy.[At the same time} you receive the result (outcome, consummation) of your faith, the salvation of your souls."

God enacted a three-fold scene of restoration in this universe that had been turned over to Satan the enemy of our souls.

I believe that Scene I of the Fall was "Adam's Lust of the Flesh, the inward desire." Scene II "Adam's Lust of the Eyes, the emotion fueling that desire." Scene III the grand finale "Adam's Pride of Life" an insatiable desire and reckless drive to pursue, obtain and conquer at all cost. "Give me, lest I die" mindset.

These very acts disenfranchised Satan from Heaven, and destroyed man and creations original fellowship with God.

Why? Why? Why?, did God allow Adam to be so stupid we have purloined for centuries? I know this use to trip me up a thousand times in my walk and in my understanding of who God was. I felt that if He were God; all in control and stuff, why did He not stop Adam and Eve from making that bad decision. But as I have progressed in my walk with God, I have come to find out that this is what makes Him God. He will never make us do anything, but will make a way for us to do what He desires for us to do; and it is our free choice to do or not do what pleases Him. If you have ever been enslaved physically, spiritually or emotionally by another human being you can understand the word free I am indicating here. And if you have never been enslaved, physically, spiritually or emotionally – just imagine how you would feel if another human being prevented you from doing something you felt was your right to do!

So, sure He could have stopped him, but if God had intervened as we say we wanted him to - then he would have ceased being God.

And what a mess we would really be in today! God would have become a Dictator, forcing his will upon others.

Clearly out of character for ONE who does not need predefined power, because He IS Power.

He does not need permission to rule, or govern by appointment, because he is the Government. Deuteronomy 28, bears this out that God set before us, just like, Adam; life and death. He tells us the consequences of following both, and then tells us to choose life that it may go well with our children and us. Remember the three-fold fall, required a three-fold counter-attack for full restoration.

The Father, Son and Holy Spirit were there in the beginning and all three had to be legally present to regain our right to the Tree of Life.

Have you ever wondered what would have happened if Satan had approached Adam first, instead of Eve? Because Satan's' desires are to steal, kill and destroy. Satan had to appeal to the intuitive part of man, and Eve happened to be that part of Adam. Remember there was only Adam, the two existed under one name. God made us temples for his presence to dwell in.

Satan knew mankind's makeup better than man. He had known God before there was man, and he knew how his boss thought about his creations.

Before the fall Adam could talk to and trust woman. God had made it so. After the fall Adam could no longer trust his wife. Today that has been restored through Jesus Christ. In many of today's marriages, the restoration has not been applied. Even in paternal and maternal relationships. Some children can not trust their parents.

Women were designed to be intuitive and Men were designed to be objective, okay! When a woman receives a man into herself [temple] she is receiving an internal expression of that husband's passion for his wife. The Word of God says know ye not that your body is the temple of the Holy Ghost. Sounds like worship to me! Let everything be done unto his glory! Oh My!!!

Satan knew that the only way to destroy the relationship between God and Adam was through what was closest to his heart. Or rather what each of them were into at the time, and that happened to be each other. Eve was the only one who could reproduce what was in Adam into the earth. They were one flesh, not two.

Eve had been taken out of Adam, near his heart, it is still that way today. Refer to the third chapter of Genesis for the full account.

Nobody can hurt you like those who are close to you. Eve trespassed the law of God by eating of what she had been commanded not to eat. First she took, then she ate, and then she became deluded and drunk on the thought of obtaining immortality, and her man having more power.

How many times have you noticed women who are drawn to men of power, or with opportunity to obtain more power. How many times have you seen men who are in power drawn to these type of women, it is all because of the fall. Are you a man or woman who craves power?

There is nothing wrong with that, but what kind of power, and what is your motivation for obtaining that power. If it is for selfish aim then power has control of you. But if you desire power to improve yourself and others around you then you are in control of the power. There is a historical quip that goes something like this 'Absolute power, corrupts Absolutely.'

Eve reproduced seed under the influence of God's intoxicating power. Through the blood we became the seed of righteousness, no longer drunk on the notion of being gods, but intent of bruising Satan's head.

We are the called generation producing the (God-kind) that will rise and judge Satan in the end. The impact of abortion, abandonment, abuse and neglect on men and women and their offspring has reached into the generations.

We have become so distracted with our own pain and self-pride that we forget to ever look up to Heaven – like Nebuchadnezzar in Chapters 1 through 5 of the book of Daniel. Numbing our pain with external pleasures, psychotherapy and internal medications have created wealth for the wicked.

The righteous have become major consumers of the worlds' marketplace. We consume more today than our forefathers ever dreamed of, and according to statistics divorce is higher at this writing among the Church, than our unbelieving counterparts.

Through Adam's disobedience, we now have the pride of life, after all he ate of the tree of knowledge; gaining himself one step closer to the tree of life.

The spirit of the Anti-Christ' was birthed into humanity and earth's genetic code. According to Genesis 3:17-19, Adam became an outlaw and a citizen without a country, a headless man -- Ichabod; one without authority, country or God.

WAKE UP WOMEN AND MEN!

For example, some women in today's world continue to suffer from a lack of leadership since the fall as recorded in the book of Genesis 2:23-24. It is time for the men and women of God to get in order. We are out of order, physically, spiritually, emotionally, financially, and socially.

Moreover, Satan loves it when we are out of order, because that means we are in chaos, just as the world was in chaos before God created order! Satan is the dragon in revelations prowling and waiting on our offspring so he can devour our seed.

Remember in Genesis how the Spirit of God hovered over the face of the deep. The whole earth was without form. God brooded over that chaos and drew out order.

When a man and woman are married, there is already a pre-arranged lack of divine ordination in the home.

Until the blood is applied to their minds and wills. Those two are not transformed or renewed. Satan will seek to steal, kill, and destroy that relationship.

Being unequally yoked does not refer only believer to unbeliever, but to maturity levels, purpose and commitment among believers. You must have something else to build on besides sex. Sex is great inside of marriage it was created for the purpose of worshipping God, a holy communion if you would of two individuals giving themselves to the other for the others pleasure. That is pleasing to God, if you don't believe read the book of Solomon. We have not a High Priest that is not touched by what we feel. Heaven to Earth! You can not build a life or serve in the army of God, always having sex and never working in the vineyard.

So, sex is not all there is to marriage, because God forbid should one become incapicated sexually. Then what?

If the house is out of order and the people in the house are out of order, then they will reproduce a generation that is out of order. This is Satan's vice grip on the nation of humanity, especially those who have turned their back and forgotten their God. They are prime candidates and targets for the advancement of the Anti-Christ movement. Are you asking how I could say such a thing?

I didn't God did, in I John 2:18-26 "Little children, it is the last time: and as ye have heard that antichrist shall come, even now are there many antichrists; whereby we know that it is the last time. They went out from us, but they were not of us; for if they had been of us, they would no doubt have continued with us: but they went out, that they might be made manifest that they were not all of us.

But ye have an unction from the Holy One, and ye know all things. I have not written unto you because you know not the truth, but because ye know it, and that no lie is of the truth. Who is a liar but he that denieth that Jesus is the Christ? He is an anti-christ, that denieth the Father and the Son. Whosoever denieth the Son, the same hath not the Father: [but] he that acknowledgeth the Son hath the Father also…These things have I written unto you concerning them that seduce you." Finish reading to verse 29. (bold mine)

We are instructed in II Thessalonians 2:1-7 to "Let no man deceive you by any means: for that day shall not come, except there come a falling away first, and that man of sin be revealed, the son of perdition; Who opposeth and exalteth himself above all that is called God, or that is worshipped; so that he as God sitteth in the temple of God, showing himself that he is God. Remember ye not, that, when I was yet with you, I told you these things. And now ye know what withholdeth that he might be revealed in his time. For the mystery of iniquity doth already work: only he who now letteth will let, until he be taken out of the way."

This scripture tells of the wolves in sheep's clothing, those that join the church, but remain on the wayside. And when things do not go the way they think they should they split the church, and are numbered among those who do not remain in the fold.

For example, in John 2:19, the prodigal son is the example of a wind tossed child of God. That scripture testifies of this truth in I John 4:3, "...every spirit that does not confess Jesus is not from God; and this is the spirit of the Antichrist, of which you have heard that is coming, and now it is already in the world."

The anti-christ sole purpose is to thwart the destiny, purpose and divine order of Gods' creation man.

According to Genesis 3:11; 3:16, and 3: 22-23 the sin of disobedience, turned over the field of man's carnal flesh to Satan.

It is said remember that the possession of absolute power corrupts absolutely. The sin of disobedience caused mankind to lose his ability to understand the ways of God, and his purpose in one quick moment of pleasure. What God had given man in Genesis 1:28-30, was his whole purpose for being.

His job description if you will, his power of attorney and the keys to the city. All, was lost until Jesus Christ ascended into heaven and sprinkled his blood on the mercy seat as our eternal High Priest.

Fallen man lost his direction, title, power and legal access, and divine order in the earth. Divine order ceased in his life, and in the earth. But our warrior Prince Jesus showed up on the scene of darkness, became the access by which we could enter into the restored place and posture of the original divine order.

"For as by one man's disobedience many were made sinners, so by the obedience of one shall many be made righteous" (John 5:19) "For if we be planted together in the likeness of his death, we shall be also in the likeness of his resurrection: Knowing this that our old man is crucified with him, that the body of sin might be destroyed, that henceforth we should not serve sin...let not sin reign in your mortal body. Neither yield ye your members as instruments ...but yield yourselves unto God...for sin shall not have dominion over you. For the wages of sin is death; but the gift of God is eternal life through Jesus Christ our Lord."(Author's Paraphrase of John 6)

The divine order of the "Zoe" life; the God-kind of life is to be enabled to live a life of righteousness. Every level of man's being; spirit, soul, mind and body transformed into a unified being through the power of the Word of God and the Holy Spirit. The wholeness of God was sealed and returned for mans' reclamation. There are no longer any shackles and yokes of iron of lack in health, wealth, deliverance, protection, and soundness that can hold us captive, they were crushed, and became as ashes under the soles of our feet.

God formed woman as a vessel of honor to receive and contain the seed of unity from her God ordained husband. Even in this age of invitro fertilization, a man-child is born as a product of this unity. In the sanctity of marriage, a woman's vessel has the power to touch and affect the heart of her Adam. Her touch, fellowship and companionship should cause him to want to pleasure God foremost through expressing his love in praise and worship as high priest in her presence.

Then in turn share that love with her that God pours in his heart because of his praise and worship.

A born again man as the High Priest of his own vessel, magnifies God in Heaven, and is now capable of magnifying God in the earth through his time of intimacy with his wife.

When man has consistently aligned his desires with God's desires, her desires will line up with her husbands. With the divine order of God operating in the midst of them a husband is compelled to love his wife as Christ loved the church, willing to lay down his life physically, but foremost spiritually – putting his need before hers. She will in turn render to her husband the same, and that joint sacrifice knits them together in their secret and inward parts; spiritually, physically, and emotionally.

Mankind was given the inward desire to make and keep God as his center. In an unregenerate state his desires are towards himself, and the approval of other people. The disciples possessed an inward yearning to tarry for that power that would enable them to remain God-centered. So must we yearn for that same power.

The Holy Spirit is the sustaining component of Salvation that causes us to do what we would not normally be able to do, or desire to do.

Like Paul, said when he desired to do good, evil was always present and that which he should not do, yet he did. Now we have received dunamis that has not been weakened with time, but gained power with time. We are sealed with the presence of God, and compelled to express a perfected praise as an outward demonstration of the inward unity between God and a born-again believer. Unregenerate man has this inward desire, but mistakes it for a need for wanton excess and worldly pleasures.

When these temporary highs subside, there is still, emptiness, and a yearning to be whole. Wholeness can only be found in our loving God.

Remember mankind had only received the spoken Word of God and not the written word before the fall. Moreover, in man's unregenerate state he turned his desires from God, and placed them on himself, and the seeking of approval from the masses. The disciples received restoration of that inward desire towards God upon Christ's ascension into heaven. When he sat down on the right hand of the Father, and began to pour out his spirit as they tarried before the throne of God; they were endued with power to become one again with God.

The baptism, the indwelling and infilling of the Holy Spirit provides the sustaining power to remain one. It is your permanent hookup in heaven, that must be continously renewed. Remember when we were kids and we studied earth science, they taught us about the cycle of water.

Well just as the rain comes to the earth and is returned through evaporation, so it is with our power. We receive power from on high in earthen vessels, and it is returned to heaven in the form of the vapors of prayer, praise and worship! Enabled to come before the throne of grace and obtain mercy in the time of trouble and stay centered and on one accord in Gods' divine order.

As a sign and result of their ONENESS, man perpetually is born of a woman. This is why Adam named her "Eve" the mother of all living. She is the internal receiver and carrier of their unity (Genesis 4:1-2).

Which is why as Temples of the Holy Ghost we are carriers of our unity with God!

This oneness is being in possession of the intent, and aim to do what Jesus says, what Jesus speaks, what Jesus hears as the Holy Spirit translates it to us in our earthly language.

II King 20:35, says that Hezekiah turned his face to the wall and prayed, saying "…O Lord, remember now how I have walked before thee in truth and with a perfect heart, and have done that which is good in thy sight. Isaiah…turn again and tell Hezekiah…I have heard thy prayer…seen thy tears…I will heal thee."

David a man after God's own heart told his son Solomon, the wisest man alive in I Chronicles 28:9 to be sure and serve him with a perfect heart and a willing mind. For he (David) knew that the Lord searched all hearts, and understood all the imaginations of the thoughts; if thou seek him, he will be found of thee; but if thou forsake him, he will cast thee off for ever in Ecclesiastes 12:13.

David said in Psalms 37:31 that this man, who has the law of his God in his heart; will see none of his steps slide. Jeremiah said in Chapter 32:39, "…that those who do these things will be his people, and he their God, and I will give them one heart, and one way, that they may fear me forever, for the good of them, and of their children after them…I will put my fear in their hearts, that they shall not depart from me...yea, I will rejoice over them to do them good, and I will plant them in this land assuredly with my whole heart and with my whole soul." God loves us with his whole heart, and to effectively communicate and access the kingdom of God we must likewise, as his creations love him.

The most fulfilling time in a Christians life is in, Acts 11:23 "…that with purpose of heart they would 'cleave' to the Lord." Order in its' pure form can not exist without

God in our lives! We have a form of godliness that denies the power thereof. The word in Hebrew 'Dabaq' means to cleave, to be attached, devoted, and to hang upon. One who dabaqs' God can be built upon as a church that the gates of hell can not prevail against!

"As the mountains surround Jerusalem, so the Lord surrounds his people. If we allow Him to bring order out of chaos, He will surround us like the mountains of Jerusalem."

Patricia E. Adams

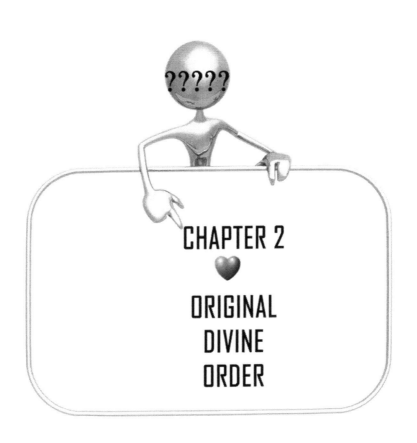

CHAPTER 2

♥

ORIGINAL
DIVINE
ORDER

What is divine order? It is the ability to remain in the center of Gods' will, dwelling, stable and fixed. The indwelling and infilling of the Holy Spirit is the psuche of God. Jesus is pouring this out on all flesh, it is the life producing breath of God that keeps the house in order. We become enabled to live the God-life, that is the Zoe life. That is being in possession of the sole aim and desire to pursue perfectly; sincerely after the heart of God according to Genesis 2:7.

What areas of your life are out of order and chaotic? Throughout time, it has required the repetitive action of conception to reproduce man in the earth, being birthed from deep within woman.

However, God has gone above repetitive natural conception, and required spiritual conception and birth through his death, burial and resurrection of Jesus. Through whom we gain and maintain access to our divine inheritance and God! Through his death, the seed of salvation is planted. Through the burial, the soil of the heart is broken open by the birth of the seed of salvation, and the heart of God is received.

Through the resurrection that transplanted seed and beating heart is pushed through into the earth as a new creation, and thus multiplying after it's kind. Becoming a member of the family of God and the household of faith!

Reminds you of the birth of a baby, doesn't it! Unless you wanted to become stale and stunted in your development; once you are born again, you have to feed on the milk of the Word of God. And then one day you become able to stand before the world, with the heart of God being expressed toward the nations.

Remember the Bible says there will come a time when you will need to teach and not always be a student! It is now required of man to be born again from deep within the life of God to gain and maintain access to our divine inheritance. You are now operating in the providence of God; the preservation, provision and governance of God that pertains to life and godliness.

The heart of God must be received and transplanted within us. We are not able to stand perfect and upright without his heart, a perfect heart.

The heart of God in Acts 11:23, in the natural realm enables us to bridge the imperfections of our flesh and enter into the place and posture of holiness.

For the Word of God says that in Him we live, move, and have our being.

He replaces our weaknesses with his strength, and thereby become perfect in purpose. Enabled and equipped for the work of God.

God gave Eve the right of way into Adam's heart. A connection from God had been engrafted into her through Adams' rib. Eve touched Adam and affected him in a way that the rest of his creation could not. Have you noticed how some women can tear men down, and others can build them up! Well that's why!

A woman's words were meant to reach into a man's heart and prophesy the heart of his vision. Creating an environment that is conducive for impregnation and production from the seed of faith. Thus if she is tearing her man down; she is operating in the flesh and psychic power. Because psychic power is Satan's version of the prophetic gift from God.

The Bible tells us that it is better for a man to dwell in the corner of the top of the house than in the house, with a contentious woman. Because she will frustrate his purpose and thwart his dreams and visions. Society has created categories, classes and degrees of natural and physical beauty. Their beauty is temporal and based on feelings that are temporal. God can take what is ugly in societies eyes and beautify them without the use of artificial substances. He is after all the first plastic surgeon, he works from the inside out, and his work is for eternity! We look at the things which are seen and become stimulated to the point of obsession over an outwardly attractive person, and once we take the wrapper off and play with it a little while; the beast appears and then it is too late to withdraw! There are beautiful people who are beautiful through and through and there is nothing wrong with that! But when your number one criteria is to seek after the flesh of that person and not their spirit, you are asking for a double dose of misery.

Satan perverts and blinds us with the secret desires of our hearts to keep us from walking in the divine order of God for our lives. An old adage I heard as a child; goes something like this "Beauty is only skin deep, but ugly is to the bone." As a child, I did not understand this, but as I have lived life a little longer, I have my own interpretation.

Just because the package looks good on the outside, does not mean that it is; and ugliness is found in the core "the bone" of a human being's character, and it is hard to miss. When a woman's husband leaves for another woman less attractive than she is. She becomes highly offended, but more than anything it creates a large void deep within her that makes her question her own beauty; and thus she becomes subconsciously insecure.

She wonders and exclaims to anyone who will listen, 'what does he see in her?'

What she has failed to realize the less attractive woman may have spent more time on her inner beauty, and thus displays a certain confidence outwardly to others than her "more attractive" counterpart. What is on the inside of a person will show up on the outside, sooner or later.

I heard another saying as a child that said a less attractive woman tries harder, and is generally of a sweeter disposition.

Now what I am trying to convey to you is this; don't be distracted from God's purpose for your life by an outward, temporary housing that is subject to change with time.

So ladies and gents if you have been conducting your own taste test by feasting on a platter full of ribs; instead of the one rib God ordained for you; then how can you expect for your life to be anything else but shambles.

Note in Genesis 2:23, and 20 that the woman was known as Adam before the fall; meaning they were one and the same, with one heart rhythm, they were synchronized if you will.

Woman was born in the image of God, from "within" man, from his inner man, which symbolizes the soul and heart. Hence, woman is an innermost vessel (Genesis 2:18-22).

Let's reiterate this passage from chapter one, that as a sign and result of their ONENESS, man perpetually is born of a woman.

This is why Adam named her "Eve" the mother of all living. She is the receiver and carrier internally, physically and spiritually of their unity (Genesis 4:1-2).

This is why we as Temples of the Holy Ghost are carriers of our unity with God!

Oneness is being in possession of the intent, and aim to do what Jesus says, what Jesus speaks, what Jesus hears as the Holy Spirit translates it to us in our earthly language. II King 20:35, says that Hezekiah turned his face to the wall and prayed, saying "…O Lord, remember now how I have walked before thee in truth and with a perfect heart, and have done that which is good in thy sight. Isaiah…turn again and tell Hezekiah…I have heard thy prayer…seen thy tears…I will heal thee."

David a man after God's own heart told his son Solomon, the wisest man alive in I Chronicles 28:9 to be sure and serve him with a perfect heart and a willing mind. For he (David) knew that the Lord searched all hearts, and understood all the imaginations of the thoughts; if thou seek him, he will be found of thee; but if thou forsake him, he will cast thee off for ever. (Ecclesiastes 12:13)

David said in Psalms 37:31 that this man, who has the law of his God in his heart; will see none of his steps slide. Jeremiah said in Chapter 32:39, "…that those who do these things will be his people, and he their God, and I will give them one heart, and one way, that they may fear me forever, for the good of them, and of their children after them…I will put my fear in their hearts, that they shall not depart from me…yea, I will rejoice over them to do them good, and I will plant them in this land assuredly with my whole heart and with my whole soul." God loves us with his whole heart, and to effectively communicate and access the kingdom of God we must likewise, as his creations love him. The most fulfilling time in a Christians life is in, Acts 11:23 "…that with purpose of heart they would 'cleave' to the Lord." Order in its' pure form can not exist without God in our lives! We have a form of godliness that denies the power thereof. The word in Hebrew 'Dabaq' means to cleave, to be attached, devoted, and to hang upon. One who dabaqs' God can be built upon as a church that the gates of hell can not prevail against!

Before God could create in the earth, he brought order and dispersed the chaos! The Hebrew word for this type of order can be seen in the word cleave, but this is not dabaq but Baqa – to divide, lay open, hatch, break in upon. Genesis 1:2 says "And the earth was without form, and void; and darkness was upon the face of the deep.

Moreover, the spirit of God moved upon the face of the waters. And God said, Let there be light: and there was light."

Without the spirit of God moving up on the face of the waters of your life there is total chaos! You must decide whose side you are on – not tomorrow, but right now! Because the further you go into this study the more you will know, and the more God will require of you. God has birthed this material out of me through obedience, and it has not all been without pain. Therefore, an anointing of obedience is upon you as you read this material, to cause you to do that which you should do, not what you use to do. I hope you have chosen to stay on the Lord's side or get on the Lord's side. I John 2:4 "He that saith, I know him, and keepeth not his commandments, is a liar, and the truth is not in him."

Divine order in a believer's life is the whole duty of man according to Ecclesiastes 12:13 "Let us hear the conclusion of the whole matter: Fear God, and keep his commandments: for this *is* the whole *duty* of man" A life of divine order will bring …"The Commanded Blessing," found in Deuteronomy 28:1:14:"AND IT shall come to pass, if thou hearken diligently unto the voice of the Lord thy God, to observe and to do all his commandments which I command thee this day,…that the Lord thy God will set thee on high above all nations of the earth: And all these blessings shall come on thee, and overtake thee, if thou shalt hearken unto the voice of the Lord thy God.

The Commanded Blessing says that,

- Blessed shalt thou be in the city, and blessed shalt thou be in the field.
- Blessed shall be the fruit of thy body, and the fruit of thy ground, and the fruit of thy cattle, the increase of thy kine, and the flocks of thy sheep.
- Blessed shall be thy basket and thy store.
- Blessed shalt thou be when thou comest in, and blessed shalt thou be when thou goest out.

The Lord shall cause thine enemies that rise up against thee to be smitten before thy face: they shall come out against thee one way, and flee before thee **seven** ways.

- The Lord shall command the blessing upon thee in thy storehouses, and in all that thou settest thine hand unto; and he shall bless thee in the land which the Lord thy God giveth thee.
- The Lord shall establish thee an holy people unto himself, as he hath sworn unto thee, if thou shalt keep the commandments of the Lord thy God, and walk in his ways
- All all people of the earth shall see that thou art called by the name of the Lord; and they shall be afraid of thee.
- And the Lord shall make thee plenteous in goods, in the fruit of thy body, and in the fruit of the cattle and in the fruit of thy ground, in the land which the Lord sware unto thy fathers to give thee.
- The Lord shall open unto thee his good treasure, the heaven to give the rain unto thy land in his season, and to bless all the work of thine hand: and thou shalt lend unto many nations, and thou shalt not borrow.

- And the Lord shall make thee the head, and not the tail; and thou shalt be above only, and thou shalt not be beneath:
- if that thou hearken unto the commandments of the Lord thy God, which I command thee this day, to observe and to do them:
- And thou shalt not go aside from any of the words which I command thee this day, to the right hand, or to the left, to go after other gods to serve them."

The patterned life of one who accepts, receives, and applies the divine order for his life is the righteous man who follows these steps:

"**BLESSED IS** the man that walketh not in the counsel of the ungodly,

nor standeth in the way of sinners,

nor sitteth in the seat of the scornful.

But his delight is in the law of the Lord; and in his law

doth he meditate day and night. And he shall be like a tree

planted by the rivers of water, that

bringeth forth his fruit in his season;

his leaf also shall not wither;

and whatsoever he doeth shall prosper…

BUT …

…the ungodly are not so: but are like the chaff which the wind driveth away. Therefore the ungodly shall not stand in the judgment, nor sinners in the congregation of the righteous.

For the Lord knoweth the way of the righteous; but the way of the ungodly shall perish."

A blessed man is an obedient man. That man is like a tree planted by the rivers of water. That man is not a sinner (oops) but a righteous man. One who practices the way of God and walks therein. The whole conclusion of God's purpose for our lives!

Everything else is the outworking of the in-working of Deuteronomy 28 and Psalms 1. Your calling and election are manifestations of your inward walk of righteousness, and the method by which God chooses to express your inward walk. Such as Apostle, Prophet, Teacher, Evangelist, or Pastor.

The ability to operate with ease in these comes from the fruits of the spirit, which is the outward flow of your love walk.

The love of God is shed abroad from breast to breast! The gifts of the spirit operate like a gauge on a car measuring the amount of gas in your car. The effectiveness of your gifts are a direct relationship to the measure of anointing in your life. Do do not get deep, and start looking around the room, and saying oh that is why sister and brother so and so is ineffective in their call.

My people perish for a lack of knowledge.

The anointing is increased as we spend time in prayer, praise, worship and studying of the Word (anointing in print) of God. (II Timothy 2:15)

I know that you have read that God gave gifts unto man as he deemed. But an illustration of whether you could handle additional gifts is found in Matthew 25 in the comparison of the three(3) servants.

Matthew 25:14-30 "For the kingdom of heaven is as a man travelling into a far country, who called his own servants, and delivered unto them his goods…Let's diagram this passage!

<u>Servant 1</u>: And unto one he gave five talents,

<u>Servant 2</u>: to another two,

<u>Servant 3:</u> and to another one;

… to every man according to his several ability; and straightway took his journey…

<u>Servant 2</u>: Then he that had received two, he also gained another two.

<u>Servant 3</u>: But he that had received one went and digged in the earth, and hid his lord's money.

…After a long time the lord of those servants cometh, and reckoneth with them.

<u>Servant 1</u>: And so he that received five talents came and brought other five…His lord said unto him, well done, thou good and faithful servant; thou hast been faithful

over a few things,

…I will make you ruler over many things; enter thou into the joy of the lord.

Servant 2: He also that had received two talents came…behold I have gained two other talents.

… Well done thy good and faithful servant; thou hast been faithful over a few things,

I will make thee ruler over many things: enter thou into the joy of thy Lord.

Servant 3: Then he which had received the one talent came and said…I was afraid, and hid thy talent…lo, there thou hast that is thine.

…His lord answered and said unto him, Thou wicked and slothful servant…take therefore the talent from him, and give it unto him which hath ten talents…And cast ye the unprofitable servant into outer darkness: there shall be weeping and gnashing of teeth."

Go figure! God had allowed the lord of those servants to see the outworking of the inworking of their individual abilities. A measure of faith has been given to every man and the anointing to multiply what he has been given, and to gain even more as you are able to handle. Use what you have and you will be given more, and that is the law of multiplication according to God!

So, God's divine order is for us to be obedient and receive life. He has set before us life and death, and it is up to us to choose. To be blessed as a result of your obedience, walk in righteousness and receive the multiplication of the commanded blessing. Which takes us right back to the beginning of what God told Adam in Genesis 1:28.

"And God <u>blessed them,</u> (Adam & Eve) and God <u>said unto them, these five(5) commands:</u>

<u>Be fruitful</u> (show forth my glory),

<u>multiply</u> (what I have given you), and

<u>replenish</u> (give back to what you have received of) the earth, and

<u>subdue it</u> (don't be afraid): and have

<u>dominion</u> over the fish of the sea, and over the fowl of the air, and over every living thing that moveth upon the earth."

Five is the number of Grace! God's Grace. His Grace is sufficient for you, his ability to work in you, through you and for you.

So you can carry out the divine order for your life:

- **Be blessed fruitfully**
- **Be blessed to multiply**
- **Be blessed to replenish**
- **Be blessed to subdue life's circumstances**
- **Be blessed to dominate over the works of Satan**

"It is time to take back what the Devil has stolen from us as sons and daughters of our Heavenly Father. Come to ourselves like the Prodigal Son and be reconciled, restored and fitted for our royal garments. Even like David who rejected the use of a borrowed anointing by using Sauls' armor to fight the giant philistine Goliath. God has ours tailor made to fit us all over."
Patricia E. Adams

"God has our armor tailored to fit US all over."
Patricia E. Adams

CHAPTER 3
🖤
SATAN

"Satan, is the author of confusion and destruction."

Patricia E. Adams

Isaiah 14:4,9,10-15 "That thou shalt take up this proverb against the king of Babylon, and say, How hath the oppressor ceased! The golden city ceased!…Hell from beneath is moved for thee to meet thee at thy coming: it stirreth up the dead for thee, even all the chief ones of the earth; it hath raised up from their thrones all the kings of the nations. All they shall speak and say unto thee, Art thou also become weak as we? art thou become like unto us? Thy pomp is brought down to the grave, and the noise of thy viols, the worm is spread under thee, and the worms cover thee. How art thou fallen from heaven, O Lucifer, son of the morning! how art thou cut down to the ground, which didst weaken the nations!

Why! Because thou hast said in thine heart…

- I will ascend into heaven,
- I will exalt my throne above the stars (the angels) of God:
- I will sit also upon the mount of the congregation, in the sides of the north;
- I will ascend above the heights of the clouds:
- I will be like the most High (take God's place).

Yet thou shalt be brought down to hell, to the sides of the pit. They that see thee shall be brought down to hell, to the sides of the pit."

I will not devote a lot of time to the study of Satan, because more than any other people (Christians) have focused on what Satan is doing and not on what Satan can not do! We give him credit where there is no credit due him, where things are out of order in our lives, we need look no further than the mirror! I am speaking of free will choices, not choices that were made or forced on us!

The one who gives power to all of us, gave him his power and devices to him. The power given to Satan by God is real, but not greater than the power God has given his people. We even falsely accuse Satan of being at the root of our failures. Don't get angry, get free of the bondage that you have created by being led away by your own desires and lust! James 1:14 –15 says "But each one is tempted when he is drawn away by his own desires and enticed. Then, when desire has conceived, it gives birth to sin; and sin, when it is full-grown, brings forth death."

The bottom line is that Satan's destiny is defined in Ezekiel 28:12-19 and Revelation 12:7,10,12.

Ezekiel 28:12-19(NKJV) reads "Son of man, take up your lamentation for the king of Tyre, and say to him, 'Thus says the Lord God:

"You were the seal of perfection, Full of wisdom and perfect in beauty…You were in Eden, the garden of God; Every precious stone was your covering:

The sardius, topaz, and diamond, beryl, onyx, and jasper, sapphire, turquoise, and emerald with gold. The workmanship of your timbrels and pipes was prepared for you on the day you were created. "You were the anointed cherub who covers; I established you; you were on the holy mountain of God; …You walked back and forth in the midst of the fiery stones. You were perfect in your ways from the day you were created. Till iniquity was found in you. By the abundance of your trading You became filled with violence within, And you sinned; …Therefore I cast you as a profane thing Out of the mountain of God; And I destroyed you, O covering cherub, From the midst of the fiery stones. Your heart was lifted up because of your beauty; You corrupted your wisdom for the sake of your splendor; I cast you to the ground, I laid you before kings, That they might gaze at you. You defiled your sanctuaries by the multitude of your iniquities, By the iniquity of your trading; Therefore I brought fire from your midst; It devoured you, And I turned you to ashes upon the earth In the sight of all who saw you. All who knew you among the peoples are astonished at you; You have become a horror, And shall be no more forever." Lucifer received from God at the moment of his creation: a name that meant shining one, Seal of Perfection, full of Wisdom, perfect in Beauty, covered in Nine Stones and Gold.

Again we see the number five (5) a symbol of God's grace.

The number nine (9) is the number of the Holy Spirit, of completeness, finality, and fulness. There are 9 Gifts, 9 Fruits, and 9 months for the "Fruit of the Womb." Timbrels (internal tambourine like drum) and Pipes (flutes or other woodwinds) with every breath he praised God, an Anointing to Cover, Established, and enabled to walk in the midst of the Fiery Stones and a Free Will.

So let's play role reversal with what Lucifer had. First his name is now Satan meaning opposer and adversary of both believer and unbeliever – nobody's friend, the seal of imperfection, full of foolishness, perfectly ugly, non-precious stones (fakes), tarnished brass, removal from the trinity and given a number assignment of six (6), representing man and not God, a beast, unfinished (suppose this is why God will finish him), and full of emptiness, instruments that condemn instead of praise, unable to praise God – can only speak curses on himself, others and to God with every breath, an anointing to uncover – point the finger (accuser of the brethren), and unable to walk in the midst of the fiery stones, but consumed by the fire.

Satan lost his free will and became subject to the children of God in the earth, and many of us don't know or act like it. Some of us are catching on, hurry, did you catch up?

I believe it is that way, and in another time and place I would love to prove it to you. For now think about it and study it for yourself!

When Adam yielded his purpose to Satan, the whole earth and all that was within the earth fell out of the divine order of God. As a result of the fall, Satan becomes god of this world (Genesis 3:11, 22-23) and Adam transferred his dominion of this world over to Satan (Genesis 3:4-5).

From that point until the Ascension of Christ, man strives for success and fulfillment that eludes him and brings fleeting pleasure (Genesis 4:3-8).

The children of man are born divided and saddled with the seed of strife and murder in their hearts (Genesis 4:9). The woman seeks to fill her void without relief with temporal things, baubles and beads. All of mankind and the earth were filled with a longing for "unity and restoration" (Genesis 4:16).

The loss of eternal life in Genesis 3:19,22 demanded a cry for a savior, and a response from a redeemer.

Satan was already on the earth dwelling in total darkness, when God came to create on the earth form and fullness. Satan had been on board left to devise weapons of assault on the earth. In an effort to stop all of mankind from returning back to communion with God in Paradise, Satan tries to woo us into captivity. (Jeremiah 29:30:, 31)

To accomplish this Satan appeals to the soulish desires of man, his self-centered motives and aspirations for control. He appeals to mans' fallen nature of the will for self-preservation, self-fulfillment and boisterous attitudes.

Ultimately his aim is to destroy God's creation by weakening the kingdom of God through wars, pestilence, hunger, plagues, homicides, murders (abortions), suicide, genocide, immorality, accusations of the Saints, and lawlessness. He uses money as the central dividing line, and the pursuit of attaining money to separate the people from one another.

These are the steps and how they develop in mans' life. First, there is the love of money. Then apostasy through the unbridled desire to have the pleasures of the earth as ones' own.

Backsliding is stepping backwards one step at a time deeper into darkness.

It begins like the steps below:

- Regression is backing up until overthrown.
- Repression depresses Gods' joy.
- Suppression squeezes the life out of you.
- Depressed from being held down until your spirit is crushed.
- Oppressed with the weight of a load greater than your strength.

When an individual falls into obsession, assistance is needed to gain total deliverance, because the object of their affection drastically consumes their mind. Evil spirits beset them to the point of unsoundness and unreasonableness, lacking any will power.

The prayer of deliverance is needed, ask God to set you free, and/or have someone else agree in prayer with you. I recommend the following authors of books on deliverance prayers to you, Liberty Savard, Derek Prince, Francis Frangipane, and Germaine Copeland. There are many others that can be found in your local Christian bookstore.

At the step of possession one should use extreme caution. Absolute control, voices, insanity, temperament is changed, and their entire being is tormented. Without man's cooperation, Satan could not make these kinds of in-roads into ones' life. When we co-operate, a pact, and covenant is made with Satan where we turn over our will and become reprobates under Satan's control.

Satan has limited access, and the limitations are on those who yield (stop by, and entertain sin) is how he gets his foot in the door, and through familiar spirits passed down through generations – which can be renounced. Because God said he would no longer set, the children's teeth on edge for the sins of their Fathers. "A curse without cause shall not alight, according to Proverbs 26:2"

Therefore his access is limited to what you allow him to contaminate.

Satan has to use another human being to evoke a curse on you with their mouth. God has given you a mouth to throw it right back into the enemies' camp. Refuse to accept it and pray that the one who spoke the curse would receive it upon themselves, which God said you can do.

Satan's demons manifests through other living beings even sometimes objects. He prefers a living being, because he can have fuller expression. Remember he has been stripped of his ability to express himself. So he needs your mouth to curse you with, so why are you letting him play you for a fool!

For this cause the Bible declares that by the transforming of our minds we are renewed. We must also make a quality decision to no longer walk in darkness, but to submit to God. Through submission to God we are able to resist the devil and then and only then will he flee from you.

Submission is walking in the fruit of the spirit and allowing yourself to put down roots, and become grounded, established in love and dressed in the whole armor of God.

This author does not seek to deal with how to cast out demons from others in this series, but to remove the beam from your own eye.

The soil of the flesh is corruption and darkness that nurtures the works of the flesh which are Satan's devices to grow and take over your territory.

Remove the beam from your own eye, so that your body will be full of light. The light that shines as a result of the glorious gospel being hid in your inner man, and thereby strengthening you to overthrow your own wicked imagination. I promise you that if you do not, Satan will use that entrance into your life to overthrow you.

You will not be effective against Satan's attacks on you and your family. The Bible said that Jesus asks us that if we are to be his followers, let us first deny ourselves and come after him. A self-life that tries to follow Jesus is a war ravaged and torn land. How divided are you that you are unable to stand against the works of the enemy? If you need to be fixed, why not allow God to make you again another as in Jeremiah 18:4.

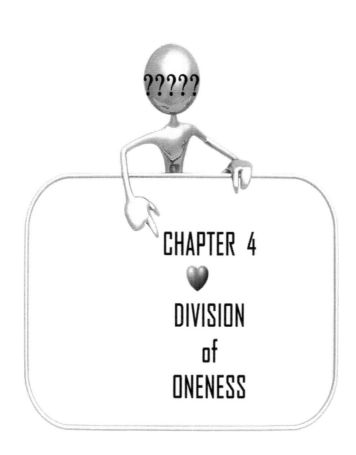

CHAPTER 4

DIVISION
of
ONENESS

Let's restate Genesis Chapter 3, Adam and Eve became imperfect. Adam for the first time in his life sees himself as a failure. Eve loses direct communication with God as an equal to Adam. Both of their desires change toward God and each other. Eve loses her place of refuge in Adam as his closest advisor, so they begin to say you just don't understand me. Which opened the door wide for men throughout the ages to tell the other woman, my wife doesn't understand me like you do. Man loses his balance and becomes self-centered. All of this occurred and more because of what happened in Genesis 3:2-6.

They touched the forbidden tree of good and evil in the midst, the center of the Garden of Eden, which was the key to abundant life. Which is also connected to the Tithe. The tree possessed the element of blessing as long as Adam and Eve were obedient, everything in the Garden focused in the center – because it represented God's commandment.

Proverbs 7:1-3, says "MY SON, keep my words, and lay up my commandments with thee. Keep my commandments, and live, and my law as the apple of thine eye. Bind them upon they fingers, write them upon the table of thine heart."

The penalty of the law was given when God told Adam and Eve to not eat of the forbidden tree, this was the seal of Government in the Garden of Eden.

Once the seal of the law was broken, lawlessness spread throughout the entire creation. Even though the passage focuses on mankind, everything was turned inside out, and upside down. Everything man desired had a curse attached to it, because the laws of the universe had been transgressed. You see a curse comes upon the lawless. God does not have to curse anything or anybody, simply violate the law that is governing that part of the universe and you reap the curse. I have set before you life and death, blessings and cursing – choose life, God said. Malachi 3:6-13,18 references the blessing and the cursing. The center of man's existence is dependent on his desires towards God.

Adam robbed God, cursed his seed and his house, and birthed the spirit of conflict into the world's system (Satan's domain, Genesis 3:3).

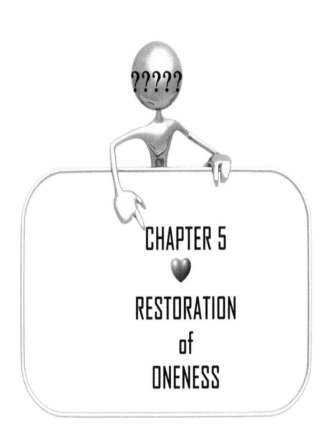

CHAPTER 5

RESTORATION
of
ONENESS

It is the breath of God, the life of God --
"ZOE/HIMSELF" that God put into Adam and caused him
to be a living soul, Genesis 2:7; that male received into
himself the personhood(ality) of God that enabled him to
subdue and have dominion in the earth. The oxygen of God
carried the components needed to bring life out of the
marrow of Adam's bones, and produce blood. The life is in
the blood, and we are not to eat the blood of animals! Every
disease is borne in the blood! We cook meat well to prevent
the transmission of these diseases. Selah! To obtain our
restoration from the disease of sin it required the shedding
of uncontaminated blood, his blood co-mingled and wiped
out the cursed blood that coursed through mankinds blood,
and carried it back to heaven when he ascended and
sprinkled it once and for all as the High Priest of our
confession on the mercy seat once and for all and sealed our
salvation. When we receive the free gift of salvation it comes
with the blood of the blemish free sacrifical, paschal lambs'
blood, Jesus Christ the Anointed One! When we receive, not
mentally, but spiritually the blood at the point of salvation it
points to a new beginning, these are they whose robes have
been washed in the blood of the Lamb! Halleluia! Selah!

The character and sufficiency of God had been in Adam. The blood is produced in the center of mans' skeletal system, the marrow. A life for a life was required to give us the new birth. But it required the undefiled blood of the Lamb of Gods' bloodshed to bring forth new life. Romans 5:19 and Luke 1:34-35, says it required an undefiled womb as in the beginning to regain legal access into this world system (Satan's) domain.

A disobedient flesh ruled system required an obedient flesh to counteract its' works and make them of no consequence. God used against Satan what he used against mankind to restore balance to God's plan for his children. God revealed himself as the solution to the lawlessness of the earth, once again through the personhood of Jesus Christ. He was God and Man in the flesh thereby able to conquer, subdue and reconcile the lawless with the lawful.

God could have done anything he wanted to do, but even God obeys the law. It would have been illegal and temporary for God to liberate us without following the order of his own universe. An infinite, all powerful, all knowing God, became a finite creature representative to enter into Satan's finite realm to make an open show of him.

Luke 1:68-79 reads "Blessed be the Lord God of Israel; for he hath visited and redeemed his people. And hath raised up a horn of salvation for us in the house of his servant

David: As he spake by the mouth of his holy prophets, which have been since the world began: That we should be saved from our enemies, and from the hand of all that hate us; To perform the mercy promised to our fathers, and to remember his holy covenant; The oath which he sware to our father Abraham, That he would grant unto us, that we being delivered out of the hand of our enemies might serve him, all the days of our life. And thou, child, shalt be called the the prophet of the Highest: for thou shalt go before the face of the Lord to prepare his ways; to give knowledge of salvation unto his people by the remission of their sins, Through the tender mercy of our God; whereby the dayspring from on high hath visited us, To give light to them that sit in darkness and in the shadow of death, to guide our feet into the way of peace."

After the Ascension, the Government of God was restored to the earth, and the Tree of Good and Evil was replanted as a balm for the healing of the nation. I like the recording of the Ascension in Acts Chapter 1, because it is in the same reference of time prior to their receiving POWER!

So, it reads "THE FORMER treatise have I made, O Theophilus, of all that Jesus began both to do and teach. Until the day in which he was taken up, after that he through the Holy Ghost had given commandments unto the apostles whom he had chosen: To whom also he showed himself alive after his passion by many infallible proofs, being seen of them forty days, and speaking of the things pertaining to the kingdom of God: And, being assembled together with them, commanded them that they should not depart from Jerusalem, but wait for the promise of the Father, which, saith he, ye have heard of me. For John truly baptized with water; but ye shall be baptized with the Holy Ghost not many days hence. When they therefore were come together, they asked of him, saying, Lord, wilt thou at this time restore again the kingdom to Israel? And he said unto them, It is not for you to know the times or the seasons, which the Father hath put in his own power. But ye shall receive power, after that the Holy Ghost is come upon you: and ye shall be witnesses unto me both in Jerusalem, and in all Judea, and in Samaria, and unto the uttermost part of the earth. And when he had spoken these things, while they beheld, he was taken up; and a cloud received him out of their sight. And while they looked steadfastly toward heaven as he went up into heaven? this same Jesus, which is taken up from you into heaven, shall so come in like manner as ye have seen him go into heaven."   One half chapter later they received POWER!

God offered up his Tithe, which was Jesus to himself, as a remembrance to himself to no longer be silent with his creation, or remain distant. Hebrews 8:10-13,9:12. Jesus seals the void and restores the "Zoe," the oneness of the God life with abundant "dunamis" power.

He has brought us reconciliation, peace, access, hope/joy, perseverance, character, and love. We received a change of wills, from "I" will to "Your" will and the power supply to back it up. We are no longer victims but witnesses of the restoration. We are now salt not poison, the light not darkness, the branches not briers, the doers not just hearers, ambassadors and not anti-christ, and stewards and not squanderers. We can then rejoice, because we are reclothed, reconciled, restored, regenerated, justified, and sanctified.

So that we might have rest, receive instruction, armed for battle, prosperous, joyful, and full of praise.

A born again believer is no longer separated by his self-willed, selfish desires of individualism to gratify his fleshly lust.

Our ship is no longer on a course of spiritual destruction and spiritual starvation.

But we are in possession of a vision, hearing ears, a testimony, an inheritance of one who has been given a mandated purpose, destiny and oneness in God through Christ Jesus.

Let's read some passages of scripture together.

First we will read about the evidence that we have accepted our oneness (unity) with the Father.

II Corinthians 3:2-3 "Ye are our epistle written in our heart, known and read of all men: Forasmuch as ye are manifestly declared to be the epistle of Christ ministered by us, written not with ink, but with the Spirit of the living God; not in tables of stone, but in fleshy tables of the heart."

Now let's read about using what we have accepted in I Peter 4:10 "As every man hath received the gift, even so minister the same one to another, as good stewards of the manifold grace of God." Okay, let's read about the outward demonstration of what we have received in Acts 3:8 "And he took him by the right hand, and lifted him up: and immediately his feet and ankle bones received strength. And he leaping up stood, and walked, and entered with them into the temple, walking and leaping, and praising God."

Lastly, let's read about the neglecting so great a salvation in Luke 15:17-24,31 "And when he came to himself, he said, How many hired servants of my Father's have bread enough and to spare, and I perish with hunger!......I will arise and go to my father, and will say unto him, Father, I have sinned against heaven and before thee, And am no more worthy to be called thy son: make me as one of thy hired servants. And he arose, and came to his father...

...But when he was yet a great way off, his father saw him, and had compassion, and ran, and fell on his neck, and kissed him. And the son said unto him, Father, I have sinned against heaven, and in thy sight, and am no more worthy to be called thy son. But the father said to his servants, Bring forth the best robe, and put it on him; and put a ring on his hand (symbolizing reconciliation), and shoes on his feet: And bring hither the fatted calf, and kill it; and let us eat, and be merry:..For this my son was dead, and is alive again; he was lost, and is found. And they began to be merry. Now his elder son was in the field: and as he came and drew nigh to the house, he heard music and dance…And he was angry, because he hath received him safe and sound…And he answering said to his father, Lo, these many years do I serve thee…and yet thou hast never gavest me a kid…thou hast killed for him the fatted calf…And he said unto him, Son, thou are ever with me, and all that I have is thine."

Two brothers of the same Father, both neglected salvation, just in different ways. If you refuse salvation you neglect it, and if you receive salvation and refuse to partake and appropriate the benefits of salvation you have neglected it.

Once again remove the beam from your own eye, before you point the finger away from yourself. Since we are no longer separated by a wall of sin or reproach!

The foreskin that was removed from the Jewish male was symbolic of God rolling the reproach off of our lives. When the Angel rolled the stone away from Jesus' tomb, that too was symbolic of God rolling the reproach off of man permanently. Who hinders you now that you do not run? See for yourself in Romans 5:21, and Romans 6:1-2 respectively reads "That as sin hath reigned unto death, even so might grace reign through righteousness unto eternal life by Jesus Christ our Lord." "WHAT SHALL we say then? Shall we continue in sin, that grace may abound? God forbid, How shall we, that are dead to sin, live any longer therein?"

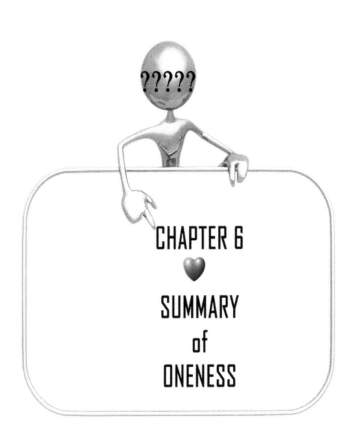

CHAPTER 6

SUMMARY
of
ONENESS

"But he that is joined unto the Lord is one spirit ... What? Know ye not that your body is the temple of the Holy Ghost which is in you, which ye have of God, and ye are not your own?" (I Corinthians 6:17,19).

James 1:27 says "Pure religion and undefiled before God and the Father is this, to visit the fatherless and widows in their affliction, and to keep himself unspotted from the world." Psalms 119:1 says "Blessed are the undefiled in the way, who walk in the law of the Lord. Blessed are they that seek him with the whole heart."

Hebrews 7:26-27 says "For such an high priest became us, who is holy, harmless, undefiled, separate from sinners, and made higher than the heavens; Who needeth not daily, as those high priests, to offer up sacrifice, first for his own sins, and then for the people's: for this he did once, when he offered up himself." The line has been clearly drawn between the sinner and the righteous, which side do you see yourself on?

In I Peter 1:3-5 it confirms the conclusion of our oneness, "Blessed be the God and Father of our Lord Jesus Christ, which according to his abundant mercy hath begotten us again unto a lively hope by the resurrection of

Jesus Christ from the dead, To an inheritance incorruptible, and undefiled, and that fadeth not away, reserved in heaven for you, Who are kept by the power of God through faith unto salvation ready to be revealed in the last time." (*Bold Author's)

"As Tripartite beings we must seek as Christians and children of God to maintain an open line of communication with the Trinity. No man cometh to the Father but by me, and that he has not left us comfortless, but has sent the blessed Paraclete/Holy Spirit to lead us into all truth. It is time for the Body of Christ to get down off the cross and accept the original way of life for our Father's creation "man".

'He has not given us the spirit of fear "the natural man" but of power, and of love, and of a sound mind.' (II Timothy 1:7; paraphrased) All of this is ours...but though our outward man perish, yet the inward man is renewed day by day. 'For ye have not received the spirit of bondage (ADAM) again to fear, but ye have received the spirit of adoption, whereby we cry, Abba, meaning Father ... For the creature (man) was made subject to vanity, not willingly, but by reason of him (ADAM) who hath subjected the same in hope.' (Roman 8:15,20; paraphrased)

Namely, the Father, The Son and The Holy Spirit. It is their way of renewing themselves in us. The Father is the giver of all The object of our affection as born again believers should be the Trinity. Why? Because Jesus said no man has life unless he hath the Father and the Son.

The Son due to the fall of Adam became the only offering, the atonement, the sacrificial and perfect lamb for the sins of the world. Thereby, closing the doors of sin and death. The Holy Spirit is the source of our new found source of life. This source is the power of God unto salvation, life abundant, divine health, and eternal life.

The object of our affection as born again believers should be the Trinity. Why? Because Jesus said no man cometh to the Father but by me, and that he has not left us comfortless, but has sent the blessed Paraclete/Holy Spirit to lead us into all truth. The Holy Spirit is the line of communication between our Father to his children, with Jesus as the Mediator between us.

The world and the church suffers from a lack of Fathers. But the worst part of this dichotomy is that the church has an exclusive Father that we neglect. The Holy Spirit is performing this scripture in the Body of Christ this hour, "Behold, I am going to send you Elijah the prophet before the coming of the great and terrible day of the LORD. And He will restore the hearts of the fathers to their children and the hearts of the children to their fathers, lest I come and smite the land with a curse" Malachi 4:4-6.

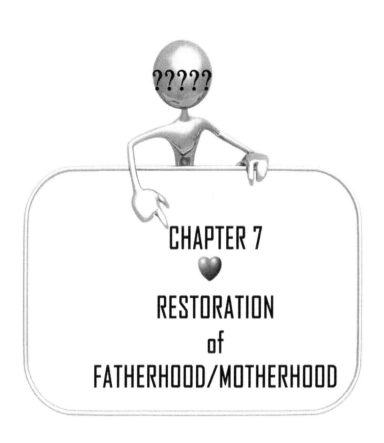

CHAPTER 7

RESTORATION

of

FATHERHOOD/MOTHERHOOD

The curse of illegitimacy can and does exist where fathers and mothers have been physically present, but emotionally and spiritually absent. I pray that as we arrive at this point in our journey that we will have applied and washed ourselves in the Blood of the Lamb, and that we are ready to lift from our hearts this part of the curse as we continue on this journey of healing. Parents have abandoned, and are abandoning their children in record numbers, but the most disturbing place this is happening is in the Body of Christ. Biological parents are gone, and spiritual leaders are seen slipping and tipping. Psalms 27:10, says "When my father and my mother forsake me, then the Lord will take care of me."

I Corinthians 4:15-16, says "For though ye have ten thousand instructors in Christ, yet have ye not many fathers: for in Christ, yet have ye not many fathers: for in Christ Jesus I have begotten you through the gospel. Wherefore I beseech you, be ye followers of me." It required a Heavenly Father concerned about his earthly children, to send the Son, and the Son to Send the Paraclete to restore the position and anointing of parenting. Our homes, children, businesses and relationships suffer because we are ICHABOD – without a head, authority! The Father sets up the government in the home and the Mother teaches the children the laws that exist within that government. But not to despair those of you who are women without husbands training children, you have the supreme Father as your government if you will look to him in that role. And men God is the Mother for your children who will teach you how to temper and balance your government with justice!

There does not exist a finite being that can fill that role like our infinite God can!

Oppression results in an environment where there is no leadership, because women are worn down by earning wages, cooking, cleaning, negotiating, and the last thing they want to do is deal with the discipline in the home. And this is where Satan thrives! The Bible says, that if you spare the rod you hate your children! So Satan is counting on you to spare the rod. With the male Satan counts on him to overcorrect with the rod and not temper it with justice and tenderness. The Bible does not say beat, or give them what your parents gave you. Especially, if it was out of order! I know what I am speaking of, when a child is struck of out anger, or beaten until blood is drawn – you are out of order!

Never discipline a child out of anger, because anger is a fire that is fed on adrenaline, and old bad childhood memories, or abandonment of the other parent. It is not a child's fault you chose the wrong time, wrong place or an ill-prepared person to conceive with. We forget we had a choice, they didn't. This oppression shows in all forms, not having sufficiency in all areas of your life in regards to your household is oppressive.

CHAPTER 8

HEALING
from
ABSENT PARENT(S)

In the name of Jesus Christ, receive your healing now, allow God to send ministering angels to you right where you are. Touch and heal my brothers and sisters Abba, Daddy, Momma right now in the name of Jesus! Holy Ghost move upon them now as the read this prayer from the soles of their feet to the crown of their heads, touch right now in the name of Jesus, be loosed from the grave clothes, shake off the dust of decay and open your mouth and confess that right now I am free from the curse of the law of sin and death, I have been redeemed by the Blood of the Lamb, Jesus Christ and his anointing, I am set free, delivered and made whole in every area of my life. I refuse to sit in the dark and damp cave of despair and dejection, I am accepted in the beloved, I am not forsaken because you Lord have taken up my cause, I am washed clean! Right now God I choose to step into the light of the "Sun (Son)" of your delight and thank you for the chains and the cords of silver (bondage) being released from me now. I am no longer a headless man or woman "Ichabod" a rebel without any constraints from the path of evil. Constrain me father and I shall be constrained from evil, mold me in your image and I shall come forth as pure gold, refine me in the refiners fire until you can see your reflection in me. Create in me a clean heart o' God and renew within me a right spirit, purge me with hyssop and I shall be whiter than snow, order my steps in your word, and every thought and vain imagination of my life, bring it under your control, I submit myself under your mighty hand, so that I may be able to resist the Devil and he will flee from me, not one way, but seven ways. Teach me your way and I will observe them with my whole heart. I release my mother and my father from any act of retribution or revenge, I put them in your hands to vindicate because you said that vengeance is yours, and I ask for mercy on their behalf that you would send laborers in their path to minister the glorious gospel of salvation to them. Teach me how to set boundaries in my life, in the area of all my relationships, protect and shield my heart as I learn to walk in your pure love for all of us. I will hate the sin of my forefathers and not them individually. I choose to by faith not by my feelings to forgive any act of lawlessness that my family has done to me, I ask that you would remove this from my heart as I am able to bear. Make me a living epistle before all men, let me reach back and strenghten my brethren when I have been converted, and to teach transgressors your way. Make me a blessing so that I may freely bless others with the joy of your salvation. I thank you that as I have prayed this prayer as an act of faith, trust and confidence in you and not of my feelings that I am no longer without parents, you are my parents in every area of my life from this day forward in Jesus Name I pray, Amen!

As you continue your journey day by day, second by second, minute by minute, mili-second by mili-second; keep a heart that is quick to repent and repray this prayer or any prayer that God impreses on your heart until you are standing on your own two feet. Meanwhile everyday enter into it with a spirit and a mind of thanksgiving, thank him that all the things that you prayed today have been accomplished in your life.

Here is this prayer again converted to thanksgiving:

In the name of Jesus Christ, I thank you that I have received healing and allowed God to send ministering angels to me right where I am. I have been touched and healed by you, my Abba, Daddy, Momma. That now the name of Jesus and the Holy Ghost have moved upon me from the soles of my feet to the crown of my head. That I am loosed from the grave clothes, shaken off the dust of decay as I opened my mouth and confessed that I am free from the curse of the law of sin and death, I have been redeemed by the Blood of the Lamb, Jesus Christ and his anointing, I am set free, delivered and made whole in every area of my life. Because, I refused to sit in the dark and damp cave of despair and dejection, I am accepted in the beloved, I am not forsaken because you Lord have taken up my cause, I am washed clean! I chose to step into the light of the "Sun (Son)" of your delight and the chains and the cords of silver (bondage) are released from me now. I am no longer a headless man or woman "Ichabod" a rebel without any constraints from the path of evil. I am constrained from evil, being molded in your image and I am coming forth as pure gold, refined in the refiners fire until you can see your reflection in me. Created in me each day a clean heart o' God and a renewed right spirit, purged with hyssop, and being made whiter than snow, you order my steps in your word, and every thought and vain imagination of my life, is under your control, I submitted myself under your mighty hand, and I am able to resist the Devil and he flees from me, not one way, but seven ways. Iam being taught your way and I will observe them with my whole heart. I released my mother and my father from any act of retribution or revenge, I placed them in your hands to vindicate because you said that vengeance is yours, and I asked for mercy on their behalf that you would send laborers in their path to minister the glorious gospel of salvation to them. You are teaching me how to set boundaries in my life, in the area of all my relationships, protecting and shielding my heart as I learn to walk in your pure love for all of us. I hate the sin of my forefathers and not them individually. I chose faith not my feelings to forgive any act of lawlessness that my family has done to me, I asked that you would remove this from my heart as I am able to bear. Make me a living epistle before all men, let me reach back and strenghten my brethren when I have been converted, and to teach transgressors your way. I am a blessing so that I may freely bless others with the joy of your salvation. I thank you that as I have prayed this prayer as an act of faith, trust and confidence in you and not of my feelings that I am no longer without parents, you are my parents in every area of my life from this day forward in Jesus Name I pray, Amen!

Ask God to reveal hurts and resentments from your experience with the absent parent. Forgive those persons; biological, adoptive or spiritual leaders. Pray for rhema – revelation of the word of God that will cause you to see this role through God's eyes. Receive God as your father and mother and accept that his love is from everlasting to everlasting.

CHAPTER 9

🖤

THE
CHRISTIAN MALES'
RELATIONSHIP

"The female is the lock, and the male is the key. Apart from each other they don't fulfill the purpose of which they were designed. That is to secure those things, which are God given to them as a family ordained by God. A single born again woman has God as her key, and a single man has God as his lock. All things exist in Him!" Don't open or be opened for or by just anyone!
Patricia E. Adams

9- The Christian Male's Relationship

A - To God

The Tithe on our time is 2.4 hours, which is 10% of a twenty-four hour day! Right? Okay, so if you feel a leading on your life to teach, you could discuss with your wife as part of your time tithe and training for future opportunities of having a cell group at home using part of your 2.4 hours. For example for an hour or less before everyone else rises you could spend that time with God and throughout the day spread the remaining one hour and forty-minutes as power breaks. While we are desiring a wife we can let God love on us, in us and through us, so that we don't seek after simply erotic love, but agape love. All love is of God, but Agape is Gods' way of loving us and others. The other forms of love are our way of expressing ourselves to those arounud us. All forms originate from Agape – Gods' love. If you love God and have the love of God in you then it is shed abroad from breast to breast and cheek to cheek. If the person you are desiring to spend your life with does not love God, they will squander your youth and time. When someone truly knows and has experienced the love of God in their own hearts, they will never ask you to lower yourself to the position of a playmate over being a godly spouse. God is love, and I know that as strongly as I have pursued after him, and allowed him to love me I can still trace the ways of the old man. Now understand we will forever be able to trace the old man, but will we submit the old man under God's authority over our own when the pressure is on. A mature christian will, but a christian who is still needing to be patronized will not. Sometimes the presence of his love is so pure that I find myself whincing at his touch. His love is tangible and you know it when you are in his presence enough. Love is at its' strongest when it is expressed through God to mankind. A lesser degree of love will fade and falter, but Gods' love is from everlasting to everlasting.

The man must be able to teach his family according to Ephesians 6:4. Divine order says the role of the father is the government (Law Giver) and intercession (High Priest) of his house and the instructing of the government and joining you in intercession as an heir and joint-heir is the mothers. Not subservient or relegated to a lesser role. You lead as God leads you, and you both lead in the diverse ways God has ordained for you, together as an unit! You give the law by drawing from God's Word what he says about your family. Train yourself through the help of the Holy Ghost to rightly divide the Word, through daily word study, via cassette tapes, Bible, local church, etc. The books of Romans, Galatians, Ephesians, Hebrews, and the Songs of

Solomon are essential to a sound foundation. Then share that knowledge with others to develop your teaching skills. Do not wait for a calling to teach. Be instant in season, and out of season.

Whenever God opens a door teach the Word. Start a home group, go onto college campuses, or an inner city mission. Then you will see how much you know, of the basic truths in the Bible. Then you are ready for the next role. That of an intercessor, as Hebrews 7:25 mentions.

As a teacher you learn to represent God to your family, and when he combines the role of an intercessor--he will be in proper order to represent his family before God.

Study the ministry of intercession in Genesis 18:16-33, Exodus 32:1-14, and Numbers 16:41-50. Then meditate on Ezekiel 22:30. Memorize the priestly blessing of Adam in Numbers 6:24-27, and make this your daily pattern for blessing your family. Cultivate your prayer life, by praying for those God lays on your heart, make a list. Participate in a prayer meeting where you can learn how to pray for others. Which will cause you to see the extent of how well you are doing overall in preparing for the role of headship.

It is not the head who does not follow the body, but the body who does not follow the head when there is division.

What's in a name? I can tell you an awful lot is in a name. When we name our children we should be very careful, because for the rest of that child's life they will be known by that name. Every time you call that child you are calling out his character, and if you have given them a name that has no meaning or some name you fancied because it gave you goose pimples – you call them a name that has no meaning.

"Among the ancients a name not only summed up a man's history but represented his personality with which it was almost identical." (Lockyer, Herbert <u>All the Men of the Bible</u>, p. 366)

When a child is named it should speak of his character, that you believe the child actually possesses or that which you are invoking into his life. Every time you call that name you should be drawing out of that child its' destiny, and they will rise to the occasion.

If every vulgar adjective, but your given name has been used to call you and you tend to behave like those adjectives – don't despair.

Here goes God to the rescue in Proverbs 22:1, says "A GOOD name is rather to be chosen than great riches, and loving favour rather than silver and gold."

So if you have been called a fool most of your life, and your behavior has become characteristic of a fool – God can reverse the curse! Fall out of agreement with all the names you have been called and ask God to create in you a clean heart and renew a right spirit, because it has affected your spirit.

A good name chosen can be earned through behaving in a manner that is pleasing to God. Keeping your word, making good on promises, being on time, and being a confidante and friend, and things like this will earn you a good name. Even if your parents named you Ahira, meaning brother of evil. God can take any circumstance and reverse it when you walk upright before him. Your name will be given to your wife, children and grandchildren wherever a male is descended in your name. Even if you have all daughters and they marry someone with another name; the blending of the two names still has an impact on your future generations.

So spend time honoring and protecting your name. You are after all the future High Priest of an entire generation of people.

As a man there are three functions to your role as head and high priest of your home. Ask God to give you the following wisdom parallel to the book of Daniel, Proverbs, I Timothy 3:4-5, and II Timothy 3:17. Before one can lead, he must be a good follower. As a result of his ability to follow. Allowing the Father, Son and Holy Spirit to be his Leader. Armed with the weapons of spiritual warfare. Proverbs 20:6, and Proverbs 28:20 says this man will be blessed.

Your time of singleness should be spent in securing a godly course for your life, how can you lead if you don't know where you are going. Cultivate these other areas in to your personality in preparation for every part of your life. They are the training wheels for marriage.

If you are married then you must submit yourself to God, and relinquish your throne, and allow God to become enthroned in your heart and he will direct your path. You see it is never too late with God! God desires that we should be trees planted by the rivers of living water. And that out of our bellies should flow rivers of living water.

Living water is water that is constantly moving through the process of purification. Unlike stagnant water, that stands still and becomes full of contaminants, and becomes a cesspool. Out of the overflow of our cups, that means what's on the saucer and the table, not actually out of the cup. When you place a cup on a saucer and begin to pour a liquid into it, and keep pouring until the contents run out of it and over the rim, what is running over the rim of the cup is what was first poured into the bottom of the cup, the continual flow keeps the contents of the cup fresh. You minister out of the overflow. What's in the cup is for your nourishment.

D- To Parents

Give in your current relationships, church, father, mother or other familial relationships and friendships. Set a course for longevity on the earth by honoring your mother and your father, even if they are not the best parents in the world. And even more so if you don't know who one or both of your parents are, and you were adopted – honor your adopted parents even more. Especially if they have been godly parents. Either way you invoke a blessing on your head, and your future generations.

Even in the worst of families, you don't want to have those generational curses passed on to your family, by holding onto unforgiveness towards your parents. Proverbs says to honor thy mother and father! Didn't say anything about what kind of mother and father.

Stop having a pity party about it and come out from behind that mountain of doubt and fear! God has a plan for you on the other side of the mountain!

For this cause shall a man leave his mother and his father and cleave to his wife.

If you are married and living at home with your parents, unless there are extenuating circumstances; such as parents are temporarily helping you out long enough to save money to establish or re-establish yourself. Or your parents are dibilitated.

When you stood before God and vowed to cleave, that meant to get yourself and your things and join yourself with your wife and live under your own roof. Even though you may find instances in the Bible, such as Jacob in Laban's house.

But you must remember in the context of this scripture it does not mean what it meant in our literal language. Occupying premises on Laban's land meant of his house, when they had children they were counted as Laban's children too. Familial customs always made reference to the root. David was born of Jesse, and so was Jesus, because the Bible said that he would spring forth out of the root of Jesse. Simply pointing to the beginning of the prophecy. This is not to condemn you, but to admonish you to get it together as a man whose steps are ordered by the Lord!

Visit the less fortunate, work at your local church, and even on the clean-up committee. Because Ephesians 5:25-26 prepares the man for the role of a teacher. The word taught by Christ to the Church made her pure and holy, fit to be His bride.

The role of husband is a stepping stone to that of a father. The two place him as head of the family. I Corinthians 11:3, as lover and giver. Making the man a representative of Christ to the woman and his family as a teacher and intercessor. John 5:19, is the key to man's ability to fulfill his relationships. Also, found in (John 14:9-10) These scriptures reveal the role of a bridegroom, husband, lover and father. Everything else the man has to give flows from the depths of this pure fountain of love.

F- To His Wife as Her

Warrior

Like Joshua (Haggai 2:4) and Jesus (Matthew 28:18), in full possession of your person, power and position enabled to take your family from level to level, glory to glory and faith to faith.

To bring forth life (Acts 2:36) out of desolation, and destruction to the plans of the enemy. And able to speak a word in due season that will cause the woman God has given you and the children God has ordained from your union to spring forth as the dew of the earth. An anointing to rest between your wife's bosom and speak the confidences of your heart without fear of betrayal. To share the vision for your home and speak it into existence. To know God through his Son Jesus Christ in an intimate way that only a friend, brother, child and lover could know of him.

Lord – Law Giver

There is a 1) scrotum, with two parts that are symbolic of the commandments if you would. Inside the Ark of the Covenant were two tablets upon which the law was given the foundation for building your life upon (representative of authority and government).

Ointment of Peace – Shepherd & Lover

The Lord is my shepherd I shall not want. He maketh me to lie down in green pastures: he leadeth me beside the still waters. He restoreth my soul: he leadeth me in the paths of righteousness for his name's sake. Yea, though I walk through the valley of the shadow of death, I will fear no evil: for thou art with me: thy rod and thy staff they comfort me. Thou preparest a table before me in the presence of mine enemies: thou anointest my head with oil; my cup runneth over.

Surely goodness and mercy shall follow me all the days of my life: and I will dwell in the house of the Lord forever. (Psalms 23). The ointment of peace makes sure that my spirit is strengthened for the task I must face as his wife, lover, confidante, and mother of his children and servant of the Lord and be at peace knowing that he is with me and for me.

He speaks the word over me, to me, and anoints me with the crown of peace to know how to draw boundaries and balance my resources so that I never operate out of my cup, but out of the overflow. So many of us give and give until our cup runneth dry. But the man God has over us as women our covering who will recognize when we are in need of a touch and refill.

Provider

A type of Emmanuel (God with us and for us) shows the male giving of all of his substance to the receiver of life the female. A mans genitals are outside of his body in a set of 3. If you would elevate your mind we can talk about this for a moment, okay. Three areas of the Ark of the Covenant; Tables of Law, Golden Pot of Manna, and the Rod of Aaron, of those three, two are represented in man.

Counsel

A man manages, he stands as the handler of the head of his family and lead. He is to protect them from danger. The Latin, French, and Italian word derivatives for manager -- mean, "hand". Webster defines man as one who handles or direct with a degree of skill, to treat with care, to succeed in accomplishing, to direct or carry on business or affairs, and to achieve one's purpose.

Might

Between the scrotum, the testaments; lies the rod of man, symbolic of the budding almond rod inside of the Ark of the Covenant, which represented the life-giving one and manifestation of life. A woman receives strength from her husbands' deposits. To me this is God's way of telling us that he exchanges our weakness with his strength.

This is why after so many years of marriage, the two begin to think as one and even sometimes look alike. With every moment of sexual intercourse, both a spiritual and physical impartation and withdrawal are made from the man, and a deposit is received into the woman. And she becomes a wellspring of refreshing to her husband.

Unlike men and women who have had premarital sex, and still have old haunts in their spirits from deposits and withdrawals from every relationship, they have ever had into their marriage from Sally and Jack. What was yesterday's thrill becomes hard to forget and not compare to what you have to what you have had.

Cannot you see how awesome God is! The spirit of man is a living epistle, with the recordings of everything in your life thus far has experienced. When God made man he made him a human replica of the order of Heaven!

For every vulgarity that has been spoken to you during intercourse, your mind still takes you back to that point in time until you fall out of agreement with it, and apply Philippians 3:19 to it and the blood of Jesus.

Solomon is our proof that a man and a woman can have intimate discourse without the use of profanity during intimacy. God has provided for every area of your life, just read the manual. Read Song of Solomon sometimes, and it will make you blush at the holy passion, and at the same time cry at what the devil has stolen from us.

We were made to relate to one another in these terms and not in the obscenities we have shouted out in the heat of an illegal moment, and even in matrimony.

The woman's uterus and ovaries are symbolic of the Golden Cup of Manna, which we will discuss in the next chapter.

Thus a man who desires to become a husband or is a husband is the symbol of God's leadership in the earth. I have heard it said so many times that a man thinks with this area of his body. So think about it! This is the area Satan has perverted in man's life to rob him of his heritage, placing illegitimate children in the earth without a clue of what a father is. Satan has used us to pervert, maim and cripple our own offspring. A crippled man cannot travel very far or for too long. So we see the order of a man is to be a son, a husband, and then a father.

Security

Songs of Solomon 8:6, says love always protects, trusts, hopes, and perseveres, and I Corinthians 13: 7-8, says it never fails.

This kind of love draws a bride to her husband. Just as Jesus draws the Church to Himself. Tenderness towards the woman causes her to blossom, and precludes sex in romance.

Ephesians 5:25 says, love is self-giving, and is the pattern for a successful marriage. Two people laying down their lives for each other. First, the husband--like Jesus laid his life down. Second, the wife like the Church lays down her life for her husband. Giving the other fulfillment derived from the covenant.

Peace Maker

When godly decisions are made, those decisions bring peace. If your entire house is on one accord, this is the sure indicator that you have set up godly government. If you married outside of God's blessings this may be more difficult to accomplish. Sometimes it may go better than other times. If somebody has brought sin into the camp, a godly decision will become a stone of offense in that case. If all lines are open and directed towards God, then a godly solution will bring peace from the other members of the body (family). Each member of the body falls in line with the decision and it becomes law. The wife takes the law and turns it into instruction for the family and takes the appropriate action to implement.

Dependable – Tower

A decision must be made to cultivate self-giving. Since, Adam's fall removed it from man's nature. It must be done daily, slowly cultivating it back into your character. This needs to be done prior to marriage to prevent undue suffering.

You receive information from other parts of the body, as at the Central Nervous System of the family. That means you are to be able to know when the house is out of order. You make decisions based on the information that has been received in the Central Nervous System to assist the foot, the arm, leg or wherever in the body of your family there is a malfunction or void. The decisions you make are given in the form of godly direction tempered with godly wisdom, based on the information received.

When your physical body is in pain it notifies your head of the exact location or source of this pain. Your family is representative of the parts of your body expressing disappointments, needs, and hurts.

As the spiritual leader of your family you sort out the information, because each member of the family will have a different perception of the problem; the females will feel the problem and tend to express their emotions, as they are the intuitive ones, the males will see the problem as an external discomfort that needs to be simply removed, because they are objective.

Therefore you should take all of the information and make a godly decision.

To do this you must be at all times sensitive to the leading of God, His Son, and His Word, through the Holy Spirit to instruct you. You are to sit and express the simplicity of the Word of God. Making it so simple the Bible says, that even a fool could understand.

Men, Stand In The Gap For Your Family.

Patricia E. Adams

CHAPTER 10

THE
CHRISTIAN
FEMALES' RELATIONSHIP

"The female is the lock, and the male is the key. Apart from each other they don't fulfill the purpose of which they were designed. That is to secure those things, which are God given to them as a family ordained by God. A single born again woman has God as her key, and a single man has God as his lock. All things exist in Him!" Don't open or be opened for or by just anyone!
Patricia E. Adams

10- The Christian Females' Relationship

A- To God

Both the woman and the man must be teachable. But more than anything when a woman is taught she must assume the role of implementor of what she has been taught in her local church and from her husbad, within the family. A woman should also train herself to rightly divide the Word, through daily word study, via cassette tapes, Bible, local church, etc. The books of Romans, Galatians, Ephesians, Hebrews, and the Songs of Solomon are essential to a sound foundation.

I will focus more on your first and main ministry as women in the home, since you are after all a wife, or betrothed or hoping to become a wife at this point.

In keeping our priorities straight, first God, Family, Self and Others. Starting out with the role of a stay at home wife, you have a lot of business ventures to run as evidenced by the Proverbs 31 woman. As women or men we must and need to start our day out with God, and everything else will fall into place. Reiterated, the Tithe on our time is 2.4 hours, which is 10% of a twenty-four hour day! Right? Okay, so if you feel a leading on your life to teach, you could discuss with your husband as part of your time tithe and training for future opportunities of having a cell group at home using part of your 2.4 hours. For example for an hour or less before everyone else rises you could spend that time with God and throughout the day spread the remaining one hour and forty-minutes as power breaks.

If you can keep your priorities straight, which is to your husband, your house and your children if there are any. Perhaps you have time for a 1 hour study once a week, that won't leave you with a husband and children coming home to find the house unclean and dinner in the freezer if you are in the role of a stay at home wife. If you both work then I believe God woul d have you both share in the responsibilities of the manual needs of the home as you are gifted and talented in. Even if you are a stay at home wife, if you can not cook you still have the obligation of having meals prepared, if you have to pay for food to be prepared. And some men prefer to cook, but that does not mean that just because someone has a preference or is the better at the task than the other that that is their sole responsibility.

Don't go deep and say I am working for the Lord, I have been too busy to do all of that and teach. Because all of that is teaching too, teaching your children how to manage a household, and teaching your husband your worth and value in the home. If you can not do that at home, perhaps he will agree for you to go onto college campuses, nursing homes, children's hospitals, and other places of interest that meet with God and his approval to share the Word. You could read Bible stories to children in the pediatric ward. Be instant in season, and out of season. Whenever God opens a door, teach the Word.

Then you will see how much you know of the basic truths in the Bible. Then you are ready for the next role.

You can be in intercessory for an hour, or less, or more each day, remember the Time Tithe, but don't become legalistic about it. If God ask for more give him that with your husbands (and wives (men)) approval. Because if God is requiring more then he will let that godly man know this in his spirit. The Bible clearly tells us not to defraud one another in our marital life. Everything you seek to do, must have its road leading from the throne of God, to the home first and then outward. Not outward first! Teaching begins with your own household.

Studying the ministry of intercession in Genesis 18:16-33, Exodus 32:1-14, Hebrews 7 and Numbers 16:41-50. Then meditate on Ezekiel 22:30. Memorize the priestly blessing of Adam in Numbers 6:24-27, and help your husband memorize it and you can in turn remind the children of their fathers blessing over them. Remember, a husband or a wife with a messed up head will produce a messed up generation. Help your husband to follow after God, so the body does not suffer. Not nag, but come along side and encourage and strengthen. Where the head is aligned with God there is not with his own agenda but God's order.

B- To Herself (Her Name)

Revelations 19:7 expresses an eternal desire from Gods' heart to share an eternity with the Bride (Church).His word ask us if we know that our bodies are the Temple of the Holy Ghost? The Bride individually and corporately has to make ready. Developing character and living a rewarding life that leads to an infinitely greater thing, "Home with Jesus." Finding total fulfillment in serving the Lord with all your heart. The same character traits that appeal to God will appeal to your mate.

We all know we want love and will be loved eternally in heaven. His word says that we should pray thy will be done in the earth as it is in his kingdom. Meaning that love is available in the earth for us because it exist in heaven. Reiterated, while we are desiring a husband we can let God love on us, in us and through us, so that we don't seek after simply erotic love, but agape love. All love is of God, but Agape is Gods' way of loving us and others. The other forms of love are our way of expressing ourselves to those around us. All forms originate from Agape – Gods' love. If you love God and have the love of God in you then it is shed abroad from breast to breast and cheek to cheek. If the person you are desiring to spend the rest of your life does not love God or you don't love God, it is impossible for them or you to love one another. A lesser degree of love will fade and falter, but Gods' love is from everlasting to everlasting.

Meanwhile your goal is to be real with yourself because God knows the real you anyway. You can not attain wholeness when you are hiding pieces of yourself in the crevices of your heart. Women, I believe are subject to subtle deceit more than men, when it comes to hearing what men are really saying. We tend to hear what we want to hear, or read between the lines, or add our own spin on what a man said. We look for what we long to hear in every conversation we have with a man that we are attracted to.

Women if you really would listen the majority of the time men are telling you the truth from the first time you meet them. But since we don't hear them and they know we don't hear them, we activate the spirit of deception that operates in denial that allows the game to be played on us. Some women have this same capacity to walk this pattern out with men. So we see, Satan is an equal opportunity player

And if you say, all men are dogs. Then let me pose another phrase I coined "If all men are dogs, then that must make you a dog-catcher."

Hold on let me finish! If you will think back to a

relationship that ended badly or suddenly, and replay the conversation you will see you were being warned the whole time. Rewind some of those old eight track tapes! Since, God has a sense of humor, I can too! All the signs and warnings were there sisters (brothers) that you just did not want to see. Are you saying no they weren't. Let me remind you that the Word of God says that warning comes before destruction! Let every man be a liar and God the truth! So let's try this again, the warning signs were there! God loves you and so do I!

A Hypothetical Scenario:

You meet a guy in a club, or oops church. You share an inexpensive meal with them, and they begin to tell you about all of the bad deals that he has gotten from women. But then he goes on to say that he is a straight player, dog from the old school. I love the ladies he might say, and the ladies love me. Yeah! So tell me what about you, are you in a relationship?

And then you put on your Miss Fix-it hat, and tell him oh you aren't really a dog, you just had a bad run in women. I know you have been hurt, we can take it slow. You know just friends and we can call each other sometimes and hang out. How about we get together next Saturday.

He says, okay I'll give you a call and we can talk about it.

You say when, what time should I expect your call, because I do have some other things going on this week. He says, give me your number and I'll call you by Thursday, and today is Monday. So you drop everything you have planned for Thursday and sit by the phone. God forbid you have his number; because if he has not called by 10:00 am or 5:30 pm, you will call and say I was just checking to see if you had called. I stepped out for a little bit, didn't know if I missed your call.

I am not going to take this any further, okay. All the way back at the inexpensive meal he told you his personal profile or resume. But you saw it as them just needing a good woman on the horizon to turn him into your man. I have heard the line over and over again, God knows we are only human and that we have needs, and women fall for this more than men; and after the inexpensive or expensive meal he gets a test-drive. Count up the cost of your preparation for this date, gasoline, the nails, hair, clothes, toiletries, shoes, lingerie, virtue, bed linen, soap, water, towels, time, energy, doctor bill for any disease and was it really worth it all. Because you will always pay more as the reciever God has ordained you to be for any transgressions that occur. For the rest of your life you are a mother and the man can walk away and leave you with the responsibility. How valuable are you in your own eyes? Is the unholy game really worth the price you paid. Let me try another way, say you make $150.00 an hour on your job, and your boss ask you to peform a task that takes you four hours to complete. The amount of value you have exchanged to your boss for your wage is $600.00. So, lets's say it takes you three hours to get through the Stylist, and two hours at the mall shopping, tank of gas, and 3 hours to get ready for the date, 3 hours to dine, and all night to unwind? On an estimate let's just say that this date took you 8 (eight) hours to pull off at $150.00 an hour; your total time would be worth $1200.00. Since you are not charging for this time, and in addition the unwinding time. Who has made the greater investment in this date. No matter how much he spends or gives you it will never equal to what either of you are really worth in God's eyes. Women God knows how valuable and necessary to the continuity of his plan in the Earth. Guess who else knows? Satan! And he loves for you to waste your time in his playground, the longer you play the more likely you will come back again or stay. This is not an argument against dating, this is a moment in time that God wants you to know that you are to think more highly of yourself and others will treat you with the same respect. All is not lost! Don't rest on how good it was for him, even if he comes calling or you sure that is God's best for you. He might be somebodies elses best if he were allowed the opportunity to accept Christ on his own and develop a relationship with God. Without your being the Clean-up-Committee lady who comes in and dust him off and drags him to church just long enough to get him saved and down to the altar, so you can satisfy your flesh! Psalms 145:15-16 answers your desire, "The eyes of all look expectantly to You, and You give them their food in due season. You open Your hand and satisfy the desire of every living thing."

Now, can we get a grip, already?

Let me quote myself by saying that, "If the light ain't on, that mean's nobody is home, so keep going." What I am saying is if there is not a sign of salvation's light, then nobody is at home that I want to stop by and visit with. No light, not my type!

I am not talking about a salvation that only works on Wednesday and Sunday. Someone who is in possession of real salvation, and it is in possession of them is not one who will mark territory like a dog at a water hydrant, or allow another dog to sniff their hinder parts. But you will seek God for guidance in all that you do. And how can I tell if the light is on? There will be evidence from the fruit of their lifestyle, the leaves are full and green through their relationships, and the roots are real by the places and conversation they like. Simply, by observation and discernment of the Holy Ghost. It is so crucial that you covet the best gifts and stay filled of the Holy Spirit. Because warning does come before destruction. If you are not tuned into the right frequency on the radio dial, you get static and irritation. If you are tuned on the right channel you will hear all the program benefits. So it is with God, if you will tune into his broadcast you will receive all of the necessities of life to walk out his plans for your life.

Real salvation can not be faked indefinitely. Apply a little pressure or heat on fake salvation and it will spew out all of the poison and flames it has been concealing. A cracked pot can't hold water, or an old wineskin new wine!

When I say pressure, I mean when you are alone out of sight from the eye of the public – do you hear or say God knows we are only human, we have needs and he understands. Oh, the Devil is a liar and a deceiver too! But God is the Truth and the Light of the World by which all men are seen and revealed!

You must know the God of your salvation, and exercise the gift of discernment. Nobody knows a brother or sister like a member of his or her own family. So get your own soul straight with God, and you will know those who are laboring among you.

A real relationship that is founded on the principles of

God will produce whole people who are not looking for a 50/50 mate? But a total mate that can join another whole person whose willing, and able to become one in purpose in the Spirit and still remain two separate individuals. One in the Spirit does not mean losing yourself and becoming a blank canvas as a person. Marriage is a portrait that is being painted in progression as the two of you merge and blend and create a unity with the flavor from both of your lives.

God said, in Genesis 2:18 that he would make man a suitable helper, and that is your gift. As a female , this is why you help and mother naturally. As a female spirit occupying a physical house, you reproduce both spirit and body beings when you receive from a male spirit in a physical house.

Myles Munroe, said "First and foremost strengthen our walk with God and our ministry to the saints and the world. (Mark 16:15-18 & Ephesians 4:12), in his book Single, Married, Separated & Divorced"

Because we are seeking first his kingdom. We learn to gain full control over ourselves, before we enter marriage, Proverbs 25:28. When we become overly concerned with the lifestyle of marriage we take our focus off of God and onto ourselves. We enter back into the yoke of bondage of self-centeredness, and idolatry; which is, self-worship as demigogues.

The covenant of marriage is one of self-denial, and many

of us want the ring and the ceremony, but not the marriage.

It is not God's will for us to become self-pleasers, because anyone who seeks to please himself, others, and not God, will be co-dependent, bloodsuckers and clinging vines.

Salvation is our first marriage between God and ourselves and if we don't accept the marriage vows of salvation, and become consummated in the spirit, then we have already messed up our first marriage. We have failed to accept our first love, and have missed the concept of what true love is and can be in the natural realm. And if we are not of him then we are none of his, and are against him. Be careful that you do not become and are not numbered as anathema, against God!

First, God made you (ONE), then one with the Father as Jesus is one with the Father in relationships. Eugenia Price, In "Woman to Woman" says that a woman should learn to be alone with God. There is a difference between being lonely and being alone.

Being LONELY causes us to leap to wrong conclusions, and decisions, because we are being controlled by the flesh. ALONENESS for a Christ-centered woman is time to draw closer to God. Only God can fill that longing at the center of your soul. And no matter how you try to fill it with other folk and other things, you will always come up dry.

Being an unmarried one-hearted Christian woman allows

you time to groom and develop your mind, reputation, work ethic, appearance, home, friendships, and spirit.

Volunteer to give divine guidance to children in your church, community and family. Share how God has preserved or restored your destiny through Christ Jesus.

All of this allows us to better understand God and ourselves, and become fully equipped to face life through God in us. Let's reflect on this next chapter.

A MOMENT OF REFLECTION

Because of deception, disobedience, shame and guilt; sin was concieved. I find this amazing, before Satan was kicked out of heaven sin did not exist. It was not until Satan found in Adam a partner of agreement that sin was birthed into the Earth. Scripture confirms that how can two walk together accept they agree! God is awesome! Satan was in the Earth and it was without form or void, and darkness was upon the face of the deep. God came and hovered over the face of the deep, brooded, drew creation out of it and gave Adam the Earth. According to John 3:19, where there is deception sin is waiting to be born into your environment. Since the fall women have been confrontational and men withdrawn and uncommunicative.

I stressed that because both men and women seem to

find it easier to talk to other men and women. We began to hide and camouflage in outward, and spiritual clothing. Cloaking if you would allow me to say so. Our spirits have so many different changes of clothes it is hard for us to keep up with all the matching ensembles.

So we hide our true selves, thinking that if we don't know each other and let the other person really get to know us – they will stick around longer. Resulting in the practice of deception, and the work of the anti-christ. We attempt to cover up our nakedness, without realizing that in the eyes of God we are still naked before him. It is time for us to spiritually acknowledge that he sees us as we truly are, so get real with him and allow him to fill the hunger and thirst of your ravaged life. We tend to mistake the longing for sexual encounters, fantasies and objects as necesities of life. Because it appeals to the lowest level of our being; that is the need for self-satisfaction. God does not need or require sex toys or masturbation or multiple sexual preferences for his glory! Let me speak briefly on masturbation. When we are in this state, and I do mean state we are entering into a spiritual realm mentally, emotionally, and physically without a covering. And all of the demons of sex are in attendance, namely one called Incubus. I have heard some women talk about it felt as if someone had entered them and brought them to climax. You know I believe this is highly possible, plausible and likely to have happened. During masturbation we enter into an almost trance like state of passion and release! Careful you might have slept with the enemy in more ways than one, and this can lead to possession and oppresion that will lead and drive you into other levels of sexual darkness. Even as men are projected givers , women are internal receivers, and even in the marriage bed an even exchange has to occur based on the order of God in the natural and the spiritual realm of life. One without the other creates a vaccuum and drain on the energy of the relationship. It is addictive and ungodly, but rest assured Jesus is the anti-dote and the Savior of every vice!

Maybe in another setting or genre we can get more involved into sexual sins and how the enemy entertains himself and us through that expression. Because many of us believe that God does not get involved in our sexual lives. Especially, the marriage bed is off limits, taboo to God, and anything should go. Because the Bible says that the marriage bed is undefiled before God, so we can do whatever we want in the bed? In every area of life God requires that things be done decent and in order, why would he neglect your sex life, when it brings up a sweet savor before the throne when it is pure and undefiled. So many married Christians are in bondage in this area.

We must move on, but what God has given me on this

matter will come forth at its' appointed time. Why would God neglect the sanctity of your sex life when he created it? But for now let's go back to what pleasures God! He needs holy hands lifted up to heaven and praises going up, and prayers being burned on the altar and feet that will carry the gospel in the Earth. We are the mobile, portable ark of the covenant on two feet. Both men and women are the Temples of God!

Any of the other mentioned is self-worship and idolatry! I long for the day when we all desire to please God in sanctification in every area of our lives, and this one thing I do; I press toward the mark of a higher calling in Christ Jesus.

Bring him glory and honor in the Earth and draw all men to him!

As spirit beings we long to be known and accepted for who we are in the human race. Through and in the gift of salvation we are accepted in the beloved. We must accept ourselves as God accepts us, before we can be truly accepting of others.

The strongest negative that I can think of at this point is fear. It was born into creation when Adam became aware of their nakedness and guilt. They had always been naked, but they identified as one person, one unit familially, occupationally and communally. But is was the eating of the forbidden fruit and the separation of their identities from God as a result of their disobedience brought an awareness of the existence of the state called 'nakedness.' More than anything else, the fear of intimacy was planted into the creation of God. God clearly tells us to fear no man, but fear the one who can destroy both body and soul. So many of us fear other's opinions of us. As women we tend to succumb and endure years of neglect and abuse because of fear.

Clearly the Bible says that "He has not given us the spirit of fear "the natural man" but of power, and of love, and of a sound mind."(II Timothy 1:7). "For ye have not received the spirit of bondage again to fear, but ye have received the spirit of adoption, whereby we cry, Abba, meaning Father ... For the creature (man) was made subject to vanity, not willingly, but by reason of him who hath subjected the same in hope." (Romans 8:15, 20)

C- To Her Worth and Value

"Among the ancients a name not only summed up a man's history but represented his personality with which they identified and were known among the family of man."

(Lockyer, Herbert <u>All the Men of the Bible</u>, p. 366) And, Proverbs 22:1, says that "A GOOD name is rather to be chosen than great riches, and loving favour rather than silver and gold."

Your name will be hidden in his name. As a Proverbs 31 woman and/or wife your husbands' name is known. Is it known in good standing at the gate because of his you or in bad standing? This womans' children will rise up and call her blessed. Because she has made their Father's name one of good standing in the gate. You are the carrier and foundation builder of future generations.

So, spend time honoring and protecting your name, not like the foolish woman who tears down her house, and the silly woman who lures men into her bosom, and becomes known as a harlot. You are the future Mrs. High Priest of an entire generation of people. Know your worth, Proverbs 31:10-31 instructs, "Who can find a virtuous woman? for her price is far above rubies."

How much is she worth?

A virtuous woman is a woman of character, strength and ability.

The heart of her husband doth safely trust in her, so that he shall have no need of spoil. She is a faithful steward over her husband's provisions. She is a partner to him, a help meet (an Azar, Hebrew for to surround).

Proverbs 31:10-31 (Amplified)

She will do him good and not evil all the days of her life.
[Will not tear him down around others]
She seeketh wool, and flax, and worketh willingly with her hands.
[Will work, is enterprising creating her own job if necessary]
She is like the merchants' ships; she bringeth her food from afar.
[Bargain Hunter]
She riseth also while it is yet night, and giveth meat to her household,
and a portion to her maidens.
[Keeps a clean and orderly home. Rises before sunrise]
She considereth a field, and buyeth it: with the fruit of her hands she
planteth a vineyard.
[Fruitful and produces extra income for her own handiwork]
She girdeth her loins with strength, and strengtheneth her arms.
[She has ability physically and spiritually]
She perceiveth that her merchandise is good, her candle goeth not out
by night.
[She knows her work is needful and important to the success of her
family]
She layeth her hands to the spindle, and her hands hold the distaff.
[She creates her own fabric]
She stretcheth out her hands to the poor; yea, she reacheth forth her
hands to the needy.
[Generous]
She is not afraid of the snow for her household: for all her household is
clothed with scarlet.
[Families clothes are clean & mended]
She openeth her mouth with wisdom; and in her tongue is the law of
kindness.
[Gives sound godly advice]
Favour is deceitful, and beauty is vain, but a woman that feareth the
Lord, she shall be praised.
[Her husband considered the state of her soul above her beauty.
Because a one-hearted woman will bring praise to a household]
Give her of the fruit of her hands, and let her own works praise her in
the gates.
[Given tributes and acknowledged]

Suggestions for Preparing to Be a Wife

(Excerpts from God is A Matchmaker, Derek and Ruth Prince)

Prepare to be a helper, Genesis 2:18 and Proverbs 31.

Cultivate your relationship with the Lord first, and all other relationships work through him. Romans 12:2, Remember relationships take time, and change as the seasons mentioned in the book of Ecclesiastes.

Give God your best time. Begin with thanksgiving and praise. Songs of Solomon 2:14.

Read your Bible before you pray.

Keep a prayer list.

Do not limit the Lord to quiet times.

Check to make sure God is first place.

Cultivate commitment and loyalty, Matthew 13.

Cultivate your own self-esteem, II Corinthians 3:18. Willing to learn Proverbs 31.

Be willing to serve, Luke 16:10-12

Be willing to adjust to your husbands' priorities. I Peter 3:5 and I Corinthians 11:3.

Learn to pray and intercede for others, Ephesians 6:18-19

Learn proper care of your body. Proverbs 31:22

Observe the wife's behavior in exemplary marriages. Titus 2:3-5

Trust God, and be willing to wait. Psalms 84:11

Set your goals and establish your priorities. Proverbs 31:24

David said thy word have I hidden in my heart that I might not sin against thee. A woman's genital organs are hidden internally. The golden cup that contained the manna inside of the ark is symbolic of the woman's uterus, and the manna inside of the life she holds inside of that uterus without which no man could be born. The manna inside of the Ark of the Covenant symbolized God as their bread of life.

Woman you were created as the golden cup that receives and carries life. Without you the earth would soon be void of people. So likewise in the natural, so you must be in the spirit – you create and birth into the earth's environment godliness or wickedness. In the birth of Eve's first two sons, Cain and Abel this is evident. Cain was the seed of wickedness symbolic of his earthly father Adam, and the second born Abel, was the seed of godliness symbolic of the Second Adam (Jesus).

God promised Eve and Satan this in Genesis 3:15 "And I will put enmity between thee and the woman, and between thy seed and her seed: it shall bruise thy head, and thou shalt bruise his heel." Genesis 4:1-2, "AND ADAM knew Eve his wife; and she conceived, and bare Cain, and said I have gotten a man from the Lord. And she again bare his brother

Abel a keeper of sheep (Christ nature). Cain a tiller of the ground (sin nature)."

This is the spiritual and physical condition of every person born into the earth without Christ. Since John the Baptist was filled with the Holy Ghost from his mothers womb, I believe it is possible for this to be done today. Because in Christ the curse is removed. Children must be trained in the ways of God as part of redemption for the whole household.

Are you a woman like our first mother Eve who gives bad counsel and cost' a man his entire ministry. Perhaps like Delilah and Jezebel who destroys men through their sexual prowess, breaking up homes and families. Or women like Ruth, Esther, Deborah, Huldah, Miriam, and Mary the Mother of Jesus.

Like Ruth a woman who brought redemption and restoration to her house.

Like Esther a woman who saved an entire generation and was found pleasing to the King of Kings.

Like Deborah who could sit in the gate and teach men, measure out judgment, and lead men into battle against the enemy.

Like Huldah a woman many of us have never heard of, but she possessed such great righteousness and prophetic insight that Kings sought her out. I want to tell you more about her but time and space, perhaps in another venue. I will give you this excerpt about a woman named Huldah from <u>All the Women of the Bible,</u> Edith Deen, p.143 "A Hebrew prophetess to whom King Josiah sent his high priest Hilkiah to ask concerning the book found in the Temple. She tells him that, because of idolatry, Jerusalem will be destroyed. She prophesies that King Josiah will be spared." Read more about her in II Kings 22:14 and II Chronicles 34:22.

My point in the listing of these women were to show that the majority of them were single and had purpose, and leadership on their mind. For those who were married, I can assure you they were consumed with purpose before marriage, and the man provided avenues for their expression. Even the evil ones had purpose on the mind.

Something or someone is either leading you or you are leading them. The choice is yours as to what, or who you will be led by. Carnality or righteousness.

Your greatest role and opportunity as a leader is in your state of singleness. That state does not cease to exist upon marriage. Because you should marry a man who will complement your purpose and you his purpose. Where you are not strong, he is strong, and where he is not strong you are strong.

Even in marriage your first role of leadership is to your household, remember the virtuous woman in Proverbs 31. Then to your outside interest, a balanced woman is a successful woman. Yes you can have it all, but in measure – one can not tip the scale in another area. For instance you occupy the office of an evangelist and you have five children, and a husband, or no husband. Your first leading role is that of mother, then evangelist to your own house.

What good are you in the field leading others to Christ, when your own house is going to hell. If you can not shine the light of God bright enough for your own children to want to follow after God then what can you show the world. You don't have to agree, but I know what I am saying is true. Sure there are those children who have falen away, but if they have been taught of the Lord they will know the way back.

Too many children have vowed to never serve God, or set a foot in church again because of parents who attended churches where the leadership was out of balance, and it made their homes out of balance.

Children being kept out all times of the night, in all kinds of weather running after the man of God, oops I meant running after God!

Wake up in here with your sweet wonderful self! Let's stretch out with this next scripture. Hold on it will be alright!

The Lord God said, "It was not good for man to be ALONE, which is not the same as loneliness. I will make a helper suitable for him," Genesis 2:18-25. A Helpmeet, an AZAR; in the Hebrew meaning to surround, aid or protect man, because his flesh is his weakness, Matthew 26:41.

It is not good for man's purpose or plan in God for him to be alone. I want to look at the reverse of the word good in the passage, the opposite of good is bad. In the Hebrew, bad means incomplete, unfinished, or unfulfilled. He was not speaking of filial relationships, but those of deep intimacy.

Man required of necessity an assistant to fulfill what God has predestined for him to be and do in God. When he is under pressure, tired and worn down, he becomes easily distracted. His wife was to be there to refocus him if you would. He created a wife, not just any woman for him in Genesis 2:23. Not every woman is a man's wife, and not every man is a woman's husband. Be selective about who enters your bed chamber and rest between Hope and Faith. Wait on the Lord and be of good couragem for God's man and God's woman! Will you allow God to choose or Lust to choose? Even that Godly man or woman can become a nightmare in the arms of lust.

God gave man his direction and his reason for being in Genesis 2:19-20. Part of Adam's purpose was birthed in his woman, his wife, which is seen in the name that he gave her after the fall. He identified with her first as "Woman." In Hebrew the word for woman is ISHSHAH, meaning taken from man. After the fall he had to give her a name separate from his own 'Adam.' Before the fall they were both known as Adam. Remember what's in a name? He named her Eve, mother of all living! Adam first identifed with her as a woman, not a man – his attraction to her was that she held a part of himself in her. She had been assigned to him as his co-partner.

Adam did not IDENTIFY with the beast of the field or any other four legged animals. Clearly God did not intend for him to mate with the beast of the field.

He identified with one who was his equal and shared in the responsibility of being fruitful, multiplying, replenishing, subduing and dominating the earth, not each other or other people. She was created to cleave to Adam as one flesh, Genesis 2:24.

God knew the requirements for Adam's mate that would enable them to maintain unity, of 'one flesh.' The Institution of marriage is a precursor to the Church (Bride) and Jesus the (Bridegroom) in Revelations 19:6-9. A godly woman will hope and trust in the plan God had before her birth into the world, that will prepare her for the husband he has appointed and he for her.

REMINDER!

How much are you worth, Business Woman, Lawyer, Judge, Teacher, Chef, Cook, Maid, whoever you are, do you know how much you are worth to God and the Kingdom?

RESTATED!

"Who can find a virtuous woman? for her price is far above rubies." How much is she worth? A virtuous woman is a woman of character, strength and ability.

The heart of her husband doth safely trust in her, so that he shall have no need of spoil. She is a Faithful steward over her husband's provisions. She is a partner to him, a help meet (an Azar, Hebrew for to surround).

Proverbs 31:10-31 (Amplified)

She will do him good and not evil all the days of her life.
[Will not tear him down around others]
She seeketh wool, and flax, and worketh willingly with her hands.
[Will work, is enterprising creating her own job if necessary]
She is like the merchants' ships; she bringeth her food from afar.
[Bargain Hunter]
She riseth also while it is yet night, and giveth meat to her household, and a portion to her maidens.
[Keeps a clean and orderly home. Rises before sunrise]
She considereth a field, and buyeth it: with the fruit of her hands she planteth a vineyard.
[Fruitful and produces extra income for her own handiwork]
She girdeth her loins with strength, and strengtheneth her arms.
[She has ability physically and spiritually]
She perceiveth that her merchandise is good, her candle goeth not out by night.

[She knows her work is needful and important to the success of her family]

She layeth her hands to the spindle, and her hands hold the distaff.

[She creates her own fabric]

She stretcheth out her hands to the poor; yea, she reacheth forth her hands to the needy.

[Generous]

She is not afraid of the snow for her household: for all her household is clothed with scarlet.

[Families clothes are clean & mended]

She openeth her mouth with wisdom; and in her tongue is the law of kindness.

[Gives sound godly advice]

Favour is deceitful, and beauty is vain, but a woman that feareth the Lord, she shall be praised.

[Her husband considered the state of her soul above her beauty. Because a one-hearted woman will bring praise to a household]

Give her of the fruit of her hands, and let her own works praise her in the gates. [Given tributes and acknowledged]

E- Church

In the church community you can visit the less fortunate, work at your local church, and even on the clean-up committee. The word taught by Christ to the Church made her pure and holy, fit to be His bride.

This is a place where few of us strike a balance. We who have once been in the world, and come to our senses like Nebuchadnezzar and look up to the Lord. We will come to church and neglect our family or job obligations and say we are doing it in the name of the Lord. We stand up and testify that our families don't understand, and they don't support us; even though they can see a change in us. We suddenly get a persecution complex, and adapt an attitude that everybody is against us living for God.

Well I would like to paint a picture for you. If you are single, and are without children – the Bible clearly says that you can give full attention to the things of God. And if you are single with children, and especially if your children are between the ages of 6 months to 18 years and are still your sole responsibility. Then you are required by God to divide your attention, by putting him first. Just as we tithe ten percent of our income, we are to tithe ten percent of our time to God.

Then take the remainder of our income and time, which is ninety-percent for both and distribute it equally among our other responsibilities. For many years I was out of balance in these areas, and once you are and you get it straightened out, the enemy will test you on it again; unless you stand firm in the faith that He that is able to begin a good work in you is able to carry it on to completion! He does not want us so heavenly minded that we allow ourselves to become lunatics, and stumbling blocks to the people we live in this world with, that includes our families. Nobody wants to be like the Jesus most of us reflect in our daily lives. But to be like the true and living Jesus is the perfect example, that says if he will be lifted up in the earth, that he would draw all men unto Him! When people look at relatives by birth, they can see a common thread amongst them without even asking if they belong to the same family! So if it is that way in the natural, people should be able to see that you belong to the family of God, by looking at your countenance, and not by what you say or what version of the Bible you carry around.

The Bible says that charity begins at home and spreads abroad, and that a man (woman) who will not provide for his or her house is akin to an infidel.

If you are busy following the preacher at the expense of your family, then you are neglecting your family. Writing so called "faith checks" and your children are sitting in the dark, ragged, hungry and sick. Now I believe in faith, I believe in vows and pledges, but I believe that God will confirm on the inside of your spirit when you are writing a check in faith, and writing one out of shame or pressure. Been there, done that and got the raggedy t-shirt! God is a God of order, and not chaos! If you are so busy looking good to impress the church crowd, and your children and your spouse are looking like they belong to the street society. You are out of order, and you must come to your senses! Take care of God's house through the giving of your offerings; tithes, love offerings, alms, and your time! I know sometimes we attend churches where we are the entire workforce, but that is a false burden; if you are doing it because you think nobody else can do it but you. If there are other people who are there and willing to assume the responsibilities and bare the same giftings that the position requires, let it go! Take care of your home, render unto God what is God's!

The greatest ministry or witness we should seek to have is that as for me and my house we will serve the Lord! Preach your life as a living epistle before your family. Many children have grown up as preachers' kids hating church, God and anybody who says they are Christians, because of imbalance in your service to God. So busy worshipping the position, that you forgot about the God of the Harvest! In reality that is not serving God in Spirit and in Truth, but in flesh and error! You went to everything, everywhere dragging your babies behind you so you would please the Pastor, or the church committee. Then the babies became sickly, falling asleep in class and too lethargic to pay attention.

You supported and participated on every ministry, but the one at home. And you can not understand why your unsaved spouse has not been converted, or your children can not wait to grow up and get out so they don't ever have to go to church again. I have seen it happen over and over again. Don't get me wrong there are those who are balanced in their walk, and their loved ones still are not saved! All I am saying is after having done all to stand, meaning doing it

Gods' way; then stand having your loins girded, and expect God to answer prayer! You may go home to be with the Lord, before it happens? But God is certain to see them come to repentance . When you have prayed, that all that He has given unto you in this lifetime and the life to come; declared that through your generations your family will serve the Lord, and that not a drop of seed will be wasted on Satan! God will prevail! He will place all of Heavens attention on the altar of incense, the prayers and supplications before the Throne on your families behalf.

God has made it so plain for us, but because we want to please man more than God, we worry about what people will think if we don't show up or put up! This choice places us in an idolatrous relationship! The greatest message you will ever preach Prophet/ess, Evangelist, Pastor, Teacher, or Apostle is the message that your children see you display to them! When your children rise up and call you blessed, then you know you have done it God's way!

F- To Parents

Proverbs says to honor thy Mother and Father! Didn't say anything about what kind of mother and father. Time to stop having a pity party.

More critical than any facet of our relationships are the bond between a child and their parents. It is the catalyst for every relationship she will ever have in her lifetime. All relationships flow effectively or destructively from this first relationship that a child has to their parents. A child with bad parents is a city without walls, a house with broken windows, a leaky roof, and a cracked foundation. We learn how to exist as individuals, as units and corporately with others from our parents.

Women are the vehicle by which all life either springs forth from or is congested. The greatest impact for good or evil are passed on, cross-pollenated curses between families down through generations are through our offspring.

If this woman becomes pregnant and has had a history of ill-will towards her parents, but especially her mother there is a wall that is erected in the spirit of that unborn child. If she had a bad relationship with her father, on any level she will project those feelings onto her unborn child. Unless she or he allows God to heal their spirit, soul, mind and body.

If the husband who has impregnated this woman has had a wonderful family life, and his child is carried around in a womb that is tormented by the many unresolved issues in this woman's life – a new generation will not only carry the baggage of her past, but the combination of being the product of two distinct individual gene pools.

Woman I encourage you if you have already delivered and are caring for a child now, to take note of how you behaved when you were carrying that baby. Do you see signs that remind you? Were you emotional, argumentative, bitter or unforgiving? Then you will probably see a child who is moody, easily startled, combative, pouty and vindictive.

It is essential that you forgive those who have injured you intentionally or unintentionally for the sake of your future generation.

Note the animosity between Cain and Abel, Esau and Jacob, Amnon and Absalom, and you see the results of generational enmity handed down from generation to generation. Note King Herod, who would kill his own offspring to prevent his sons from succeeding him and becoming greater than he. Those he chose to allow to live he relegated to lesser roles in his kingdom.

Join me in the following prayers:

"Father, I come in the name of Jesus to plead His blood on my life and on all that belongs to me and on all over which you have made me a steward.

I plead the blood of Jesus on the portals of my mind, my body (the temple of the Holy Spirit), my emotions and my will. I believe that I am protected by the blood of the Lamb that gives me access to the Holy of Holies.

I plead the blood on my children, born or unborn, my grandchildren and their children and on all those whom You have given me in this life. Lord, You have said that the life of the flesh is in the blood. Thank You for this blood that has cleansed me from sin and sealed the New Covenant, of which I am a partaker. In Jesus' name, Amen."

Now LET'S LET GO OF THE PAST

"Father, I realize my helplessness in saving myself, and I glory in what Christ Jesus has done for me. I let go—put aside all past sources of my confidence—counting them worth less than nothing, in order that I may experience Christ and become one with Him

Lord, I have received Your Son, and He has given me the authority (power, privilege and right) to become Your child.

I unfold my past and put into proper perspective those things that are behind. I have been crucified with Christ, and I no longer live, but Christ lives in me. The life I live in the body, I live by faith in the Son of God, Who loved me and gave himself for me. I trust in You, Lord with all my heart and lean not on my own understanding. In all my ways I acknowledge You, and You will make my path straight.

I want to know Christ in the power of His ressurection and the fellowship of sharing in His sufferings, becoming like Him in His death, and so, somehow, to attain to the ressurection from the dead. So, whatever it takes, I will be one who lives in the fresh newness of life of those who are alive from the dead. Get out of that cemetery full of dead mens' bones!

Not natural mind perfection, the kind of perfection I am speaking of comes from the seed of the divine nature that has been planted in us at the point of salvation. That seed is perfectly complete, lacking nothing. What activates it is the water of the Word of God, and it grows up into maturity and refuses to live and exhibit childish behavior. The proof is in the disciple that proclaimed that, 'when I was a child I spake as a child.' Now that the perfect man lives in me and has made me the righteousness of God through Christ Jesus. Let the redeemed of the Lord say so, I have been redeemed!

I haven't learned all I should, but I keep pressing toward that day when I will finally become so transparent that He is reflected out of me and into the darkness like Paul. The scripture says that when he passed by his shadow cast over the people and they were healed! If Paul can get there and he did, then so can I! I am bringing all of my energy to bear on this one thing: Regardless to what lies behind me, I look forward to what lies ahead. I strain to reach the end of the race and receive the prize for which You are calling me up to heaven because of what Christ Jesus did for me. In His name I pray, Amen." Both prayers are excerpted from "Prayers that Avail Much, Volume 3, Germaine Copeland."

G- To Her Husband as His

Edifier

Build on your man of God, make sure his armor and coat of mail is in place. The desire of praise has to inhabit the praises of his people as children of God. So is praise to a man, he will inhabit where he is praised, after all he is in his Father's image. God demonstrates his greatness as we praise him. So, men thrive when they are praised. It is like pouring water on a flower and watching it blossom. No one can tear a man down like a woman, or be anointed to build him up like his own wife.

Glory

A woman is her husband's crowning Glory, when others look at his wife and she is well cared for, even if on a low budget – it speaks highly of the man. So rebelling because you can't have a $200 plus dress and wearing a dress with a rip in it to get back at him, and withholding yourself from him is not doing either of you any good. I will tell you what it is though, witchcraft!

Elect Lady

As his elect lady you are chosen by your husband, just as Jesus chose us. The man who has chosen to give and place his name upon you, as his AZAR, the one who surrounds him. Will one day reproduce the fruit of your loins through her womb of life.

Receptacle of Peace

As a man releases his sperm into a woman, and her well has received that expression of unity into herself, he becomes at peace. But when a woman is fantasizing about someone else she opens up the marriage bed to familiar and unclean spirits that create a receptacle of rejection. Spirits that create false illusions. This is for both men and women. Men don't think that because it is listed here that it does not apply to you too, because it does; fantasizing about another person period opens up that door.

The ointment of peace makes sure that my spirit is strengthened for the task I must face as his wife, lover, confidante, and mother of his children, as a servant of the Lord I can be at peace knowing that he is with me and for me.

He speaks the word over me, to me, anoints and his covering of authority crowns me with peace and an assurance that boundaries exist and balances my resources spiritually and physically, so that I never operate out of my cup, but out of the overflow.

So many of us give until our cup runs dry, but the God ordained husband covers us, and recognizes when we need to be restored and refreshed. Likewise the woman is to know these things about her husband. It is called due benevolence in the Bible.

Distributor

Takes what has been brought into the treasury of the house and makes it work to meet the needs of the household.

Confidante

A woman who can be trusted will receive great blessings from the hand of her husband.

Reins

Able to bring balance and insight into the affairs of the daily business of being a provider.

Garden

"A garden inclosed is my sister, my spouse; a spring shut up, a fountain sealed" (4:12). Being inclosed is symbolic of being exclusive and private, not for public use. She is exclusively for her husbands pleasure and satisfaction. She is chaste and set aside for her one and only Lover in the Covenant of Marriage.

Wellspring

She is a garden inclosed, a wellspring shut, and sealed –

which is always fresh, clean and refreshing. Numbers 19:15, says "…every open vessel, which hath no covering bound upon it, is unclean." It is a publicly used vessel, exposed to all types of bacteria, and could spill out and contaminate surrounding areas. She is as a refreshing drink of ice water on a hot day to her husband.

Praise

A woman who is a garden and wellspring to her husband, is her husband's praise. He speaks of her in high regards before all.

Spiritual Helper

She can be trusted with his vision. He knows she is not against him.

Prophetess

You in turn take his vision and speak it into existence. Speaking into his heart, reminding him that the vision will speak and not lie. Encouraged he continues to pursue the things of God.

CHAPTER 11

🖤

A ONE-HEARTED
CHRISTIANS' SEXUALITY

"The female is the lock, and the male is the key. Apart from each other they don't fulfill the purpose of which they were designed. That is to secure those things, which are God given to them as a family ordained by God. A single born again woman has God as her key, and a single man has God as his lock. All things exist in Him!" Don't open or be opened for or by just anyone!
Patricia E. Adams

11- A One-hearted Christian's Sexuality

A - Chastity

A virgin is one whom has set themselves apart since birth and the age of accountability, and remains so until the union of marriage; exclusively for their mate.

I would like to discuss this in a broader sense with you, because there are some of you who will read this and feel condemnation or shame. Once again the purpose of writing this book is to bring healing to those areas of your life that have been hidden in pain.

Someone reading this book will have been raped and feel they are no longer a virgin. I may rattle a few people with my next statement, but this is what God has given me and I will stand firm on it.

Rape is a heinous and violent act. It violates a woman to the core of her being. And this is not the forum to address this issue fully. I speak to you as one that has experienced the healing power of God in this area of my life! This subject is one that I take very seriously, and find very disheartening when anyone cries out rape as a means to an end to get back at a man on any level. It is difficult enough for a woman or man to face such acts in isolation, but to have to have your integrity and intentions examined as if you were the one who committed the act is traumatic. God brought me through as always. So women and men I speak frankly when I discuss this matter, if you were not raped don't destroy someone elses' life as a means of revenge, it makes it hard for true rape victims to come forward and expect to receive justice.

As women we must take some accountability for the situations that we put ourselves in when we display taunting and visible body parts to a society that is overstimulated by sexually explicit material 24/7. If you would not take a baby and lay it in the middle of a street with an oncoming car headed towards it and expect or hope that the car will stop and not run over your baby. Then you must understand once you are involved in a moment where you are performing all types of sexual acts on that man and to the point of arousal and you have no intention of gratifying what you started, this is far from being what God speaks about as rape in the Bible. He gives an example with Tamar, David's daughter. At no time did the Bible record that Tamar was being seductive towards her brother, she begged and pleaded for her virtue and it was stolen against her wishes.

False accusations of rape that are running rampant in our society are a form of spiritual castration stemming from the Jezebel Spirit. And for this cause many men are sitting behind bars today, because the whole truth may have not been revealed and the evidence only began from the point of your perception. Since two parties are involved in this act, one willing and another unwilling; I believe both should be heard. And the truth will speak for itself. That is the way a righteous judge would handle it. Neither party should testify in front of the other, each should be allowed to testify in the absence of the other party in front of the jury or judge without interference. Then the Lawyers could try the case based on the facts and not what will get either client justice.

Because in this society, any attempt to portray a man as a caring father or role model are rarely editorialized or publicized. But the lewd and excessive behavior of those who portray women as whores and loose women and nothing more than objects for their pleasure, desensitize men and women. Creates a sense of I can do and dress and behave in any way I want to and no one had better percieve me as a whore or loose woman. This is contradictory. I did not experience rape because of how I was dressed, I was fully clothed, but in the mind of a sick and demented person who sees what they want and is lawless in nature, and without self-control, or intention of taking the word no for an answer, rape is their solution.

So, truly being raped, meaning you were in no way, at any point during the attack in agreement physically or emotionally – then you are still a virgin in God's eyesight.

If you seduced or were seduced by someone and you were consenting and in full possession of your mind, will, emotions and body; this is not the form of rape as I am speaking of. This can be taken as date rape or spousal rape. It turned into rape at some point when you were no longer a full participant. Which should be considered into evidence.

Understand me now; the act of rape is a violent and heinous attack on another human being by a human being. I know for which I speak.

Because of the magnitude of emotions and physical duress this act entails, the river of reason has in my opinion been quite clouded and allowed to remain clouded without clarification of the act.

Let me give you a few biblical cases of the rape I am referring to:

When Tamar was raped by her brother.

When Lot was raped by his daughters

I based my explanation on these two cases. Since I am not writing about rape, but rather chastity I would like to discontinue this flow of thought for the purpose of getting back on course with the topic of chastity.

To be -
Chaste is defined as follows in Webster's dictionary:
- A) Primarily implies a refraining from acts or even thoughts or desires that are not virginal or not sanctioned by marriage. Vows to maintain chaste until marriage. It also means to be pure, modest and decent.

Pure is defined as follows in Webster's dictionary:
- A) Implies innocence and absence of characteristics of dress or behavior unbefitting one who is pure and chaste. Dressed modestly and stylish.

Modest is defined as follows in Webster's dictionary:
- A) Stresses absence of characteristics of dress or behavior unbefitting one who is pure and chaste.

Decent is defined as follows in Webster's dictionary:
- A) Stresses regard for what is considered seemly or proper.

If you have accepted Jesus as your Lord and Savior since you lost your physical virginity; then I want you to listen to what God shared with me; "Old things are passed away, and behold all things have become new."

If I am maintaining myself in a chaste manner since I believed on God; whether my virginity from my natural birth was taken or freely given; I have been restored.

The time to give up is not now; God does not care about what you did in the past, but what you are doing in the right here and now. And plan to do in the future to show him that you belong exclusively to Him from this point on.

I know some of you who are having difficulty with this train of thought. You are saying this is not for me and will never work for me. But I challenge you that even if you slipped the day before or the minute before you were on your way to church, it is not too late to become renewed and transformed in your mind. Moreover, the area of sex that the enemy has lorded over you as a weakness; can be turned into one of your strengths. I know from whence I speak. God told me that he would exchange my weakness for His strength. And He did not fail me!

Just ask God in your own words and pray daily, moment by moment; minute by minute and second by second stand on this scripture [this is what I had to do to get to the point of having my mind renewed and strengthened. I wanted God's best for my life in every area of my life. From promiscuity to the Kings Chamber. I am his and he is mine!

When you are finished asking God in your own words pray this scripture as a prayer. This is the scripture that God gave me and I used it as a prayer for myself. In 1989 and early 1990, God began drawing me out of my mess of tangled lies and relationships. I would not answer His call until he confronted me one morning in the middle of illegal sex, by pulling back the roof of my house off as I laid there on my back and had an open vision. I saw into heaven and a great throne with him seated and leaning over, looking down at me. He asked me this question that shook me to the core, and I quote this is what was asked, "Is that how you want me to find you when I return?" I shook and cried not from what I was doing, but from an awareness of his presence in the room looking at my sin. I was ashamed and immediately stopped, there was no, hesitancy, no wait a minute God, let me finish. It was over right then and there and the fellow had to go! I hurried to the shower and kept looking up and tried to huddle in a corner and cover myself. I scrubbed and I cried some more, and looked up some more. I thought that day was the day my soul would be required of me. When I could not shower any longer. I sat down in my room, and there was a distinct odor that I will never forget. He then told me that instead of a sweet smelling savor coming up before him, that the odor I smelled for the first time was what he was smelling! It is not an odor that is equated with the throws of sex. It was a decaying and deadly odor that I have never smelt before.

He drew my attention to the bed that I had shared illegally for unmarried intercourse. My bed was defiled and what I was smelling was the scent it carried up to God's nostrils. I discarded my entire bedroom set as a covenant before God, and slept on the floor until it was replaced. I made a decision that day whose side was I on. I could not blame a faulty Pastor for my acts of sexual immorality. I had to count up the cost, right then and there. He took me to the Word of God and pointed me to I Kings 18:21(b) "How long halt ye between two opinions? If the Lord be God, follow him: but if Baal, then follow him. And the people answered him not a word." He demanded an answer of me, because at that time in my life I knew better I was in a backslidden condition. When the man of God faltered, I faltered; and later understood why. I was not looking to God as the Author and Finisher of my Faith. If the Preacher said it was so, it was so! I did not study the Word of God as I should have for myself. Right there on the spot I had to give an account for myself. I had been invited to this one church where my friends were going, and I had declined so many times. I did not want to go to any church anytime soon. God told me to call and tell them that I was coming and could they give me directions. I did! And I asked him that if this was the Sunday that I was to come back to the fold, and that if I had ran out of mercy and excuses then give me a sign when I get there. I don't recommend doing this, asking for a fleece or toying with God! I thank Him for not being harsh on me, looking back on that day. I prepared myself for church on that Saturday, as I had been taught to lay your clothes out the day before. I dreaded that day, because I knew it was all over for me. I arrived at the church and sat in the pew, and the Preacher began to preach and I heard the words "Choose who you will serve", that was what I had asked God for. And before I knew it I was on my feet at the altar, coming home and I have been home every since!

That was late 1992, I have been a called minister since 1993 and took a journey second by second, day by day with my big brother Jesus. Below is a prayer that I prayed on this journey and will continue to pray until he comes for me. As a set apart one-hearted christian woman [even if you have never had sex; it will strengthen you to pray this too] Many times I prayed this prayer every second, as my flesh would scream out for sexual gratification. Join me…

Psalms 51:1-13 (Amplified Bible)

Father in the Name of Jesus "Have MERCY upon me, O God, according to your steadfast love; according to the multitude of your tender mercy and loving-kindness blot out my transgressions. Wash me thoroughly [and repeatedly] from my iniquity and guilt and cleanse me and make me wholly pure from my sin! For I am conscious of my transgressions and I acknowledge them; my sin is ever before me. Against You, You only, have I sinned and done that which is evil in Your sight, so that You are justified in Your sentence and faultless in Your judgment. Behold, I was wrought forth in [a state of] iniquity; my mother was sinful who conceived me [and I too am sinful] Behold, You desire truth in the inner being; make me therefore to know wisdom in my innermost heart. Purify me with hyssop, and I shall be clean [ceremonially]; wash me, and I shall be [in reality] be whiter than snow.

Make me to hear joy and gladness and be satisfied; let the bones, which You have broken rejoice. Hide your face from my sins and blot out all my guilt and iniquities. Create in me a clean heart, O God and renew a right, persevering, and steadfast spirit within me. Cast me not away from Your presence and take not Your Holy Spirit from me. Restore to me the joy of Your salvation and uphold me with a willing spirit. Then I will teach transgressors your ways, and sinners will be converted and return to you." Amen !!!

My Dear Sisters and Brothers,

After becoming God conscious and aware of his ever presence as Jehovah Shammah, I began to renew my mind and lose my sin consciousness. Then he began to Sanctify me as Jehovah M'Kaddesh, with I Thessalonians 5:23; "And the very God of peace sanctify you wholly; and I pray God your whole spirit and soul and body be preserved blameless unto the coming of our Lord Jesus Christ." The he sealed me as El Shaddai, with Jude 1:24 "Now unto him that is able to keep you from falling, and to present you faultless before the presence of his glory with exceeding joy. To the only wise God our Savior, be glory and majesty, dominion and power, both now and ever. Amen" Seconds turned into minutes, minutes turned into hours and hours into days and days into months and months into years of his powerful presence, sanctification and might keeping me as I desire to be kept. Chaste and wholly His, until my earthly Husband finds me!

There is so much more that I want to tell you, but in the essence of space I must refrain. I will tell you this much, that I went through my life and recalled every name of every person that I had ever been with consentually and non-consentually, and went through a process of purification. I would be driving down the street and that person would come across my mind, I would take that name and myself before the throne of grace and receive mercy in my time of need. I would ask God to wash me, cleanse me, purify me and erase the very presence, the very odor of the person from me internally. I asked for a womb that would be a refreshing well spring to my future mate. I did this not once, but as often as Satan would push that rewind button. One day I knew I was making progress and getting stronger, because I would no longer think of that person and Satan would no longer push rewind, but hold on up would pop another name and face, and I would take them through the same process. It was like candy in a pez dispenser. Deal with that one and then the next one. Well all I know is that God is able to do exceeding and abundantly above what I could ask or think in my life. He delivered me from them and my self gratification! To God be the Glory! Trust Him, not me, Trust HIM, He is no respecter of persons, he will do the same for you. Take it a second at a time! How do you eat an elephant? A bite at a time! This is a universal God, with a universal deliverance, this applies to both of you, male and female!

You will find that the sacrifice of remaining chaste before God, rewarding to both you and your future mate.

Your sister in her Father's service!,

P. E. Adams

P.S. Looking forward to sanctified relations with my husband and making my boast in the Lord!

B- But God!

God in his infinite wisdom and desires to be one with us has made a way of escape for those who have experienced illegal sex. Whether it was by consent or violation, God has a plan.

As a single Christian desiring to be one-hearted before God we are often faced with thoughts of past sexual experiences when we make a declaration of chastity. And for those who have tasted and participated in forbidden sex, you are forever reminded of your sexual past. You can remember being entwined with another person intimately. But as a Christian who desires to be one in all areas of your life your sexuality has to be and should be controlled by the Spirit of God dwelling in you.

It will seem to those who are divorced, unmarried or widowed or just recently broken up from an ungodly union that you will die without sex. The Devil would have you believe that, but God is alive forever more! I am telling you that a life of celibacy is ordained for the Christian desiring total oneness with God.

Yes and Amen!!!

If I had to paraphrase a scripture to drive this point home, 'no heavy kissing, petting, rubbing or self-indulgence or embracing should separate you from the love of God! What!! That's right!, that is not suppose to separate you from the love of God, passion is ordained by God, because he too feels passionately about his creations.

C- Godly Passion a Blood Covenant

Godly passion is reserved for the marriage bed. In the book of Genesis when God had completed some of his greatest works, he said "that it was good, and very good." Why do you think Satan makes you believe that what God ordained for you inside of marriage, is a necessity outside of marriage.

Because he is the father of lies, I believe with all my heart, and knowledge of what God is, and desires for his people, is passion in every area of our lives. Many who have never been married in the natural to saved, born again, spirit-filled mates have yet to experience true passion.

The Song of Solomon is an awesome example of unconditional, holy passion. This passion describes God's love for his Church, by using a metaphor between a couple whom are on a journey of discovery.

The proper order of your sexuality is that a husband is to know a wife, and he enters into her and she receives him into herself. At the point of penetration the hymen ruptures, and blood is shed and a blood covenant is made between a husband and a wife. Her name has been kept in tact.

But if you think about how many people you have been with men and women, and how many of them are carrying your name spiritually it will shake you out of your slumber and easy ways.

The *Hymen* is a sheath that holds together the two walls of a woman's vagina. It is located at the base, the foundation the entrance into life, and into the world. As the blood co-mingles with the fluids of life a spiritual conversation is being spoken. It is also symbolic of a curtain, like the vail of the temple if you would, as it requires the shedding of blood to enter into the holy of holies. This is worship people, pure worship! Saying, I am his, and he is mine – I vow to be your source of replenishing and bearer of your life, to honor you will all of my substance from the woman's part. The man is vowing to cover you at your weakest point, and to render to you the necessary source of life, to hold you close, and become the watchman on the wall. If you don't believe me, let's go to the word.

First, Song of Solomon 5:1-4, I AM come into my garden, my sister, *my* spouse: I have gathered my myrrh with my spice; I have eaten my honeycomb with my honey; I have drunk my wine with my milk; eat, O friends; drink, yea, drink abundantly, O beloved. I sleep, but my heart waketh: it *is* the voice of my beloved that knocketh, *saying*, Open to me, my sister, my love, my dove, my undefiled: for my head is filled with dew, *and* my fingers *with* sweet smelling myrrh, upon the handles of the lock." Song of Solomon 6:9 "My dove, my undefiled is but one; she is the *only* one of her mother, she *is* the choice *one* of her that bare her. The daughters saw her, and blessed her; year, the queens and the concubines, and they praised her."

Hebrews 13:4 "Marriage *is* honourable in all, and the bed undefiled: but whoremongers and adulterers God will judge." Remember it doesn't matter what is behind you, but before you. In Christ all things have become new, and old things have passed away. You have been restored no matter what anybody says. You start over at the point of salvation. If God designed you so meticulously and left not a single thing undone, surely he is able to restore your sexuality. After all he owns the patent on the original, surely he can restore what he has made. Jeremiah thought so, in chapter 18, verse 4. Whose report will you believe!

I shall believe the report of the Lord!

Eugenia Price, quoted a Missionary in her book "Woman to Woman, who never married as having said, "Well, being married is <u>one</u> circumstance of the Christian life and being single hearted (one-hearted) is <u>another</u> circumstance of the Christian life." If God is in control, all things are possible, and if he is not in control nothing is possible. (*bold mine)

As a one-hearted Christian who may be in the state of singleness God is your Bank of Gibraltar; your inexhaustible source for your every need. You will not find a greater lover, friend, confidante, all in all, above all and around all; because when you rely on the natural folk to be all of this they leave, let you down and disappoint you; but not Him!

Are you praising him yet! The one who hears you, is touched by your cry, moans and groans, feels what you feel, rejoices when you rejoice! Giver of every good and perfect gift, somebody shout Halleluia!

Many one-hearted women believe that they are misfits, and have no where to fit in. But a one-hearted woman was the first to commune with Jesus' body, the first to tell the Good News (Gospel) to others.

A one-hearted woman divinely betrothed to Yahweh as husband, gave birth to Emmanuel, the name of one we call Jesus. God has a plan for you and your sexuality to belong to him as his betrothed, so that you can go to a pure level of passion. That only comes from being intimate with him, through reading your word, praying, meditating, and talking to him. He said that he will keep those who desire to be kept, He is not a liar like those people who serve Satan you have been involved with.

He said in the Bible, let every man be a liar, and He the truth. He is not short concerning his promises, nor void of memory that he forgets. Stop acting like the, widow Zarepheth, waiting to die, but act like the woman at the well who dranked of his living water, and go tell somebody, anybody, everybody to come see a man who knows all of your downfalls and still wants to be your mate, mend your hurts, and embrace your spirit.

(I Corinthians 7:32-35).

D- Loneliness versus Aloneness

Eugenia Price, said "In every life there is <u>aloneness</u>...this is normal...the secret is that we can come to the place of realization that we are created this way." (Woman to Woman, pp. 148-149)

God has reserved a place for Himself only, down in the very center of our beings. And our trouble springs from the fact that we try to fill this place with other things and other people. It is reserved for Christ himself, nothing else will fit, and we must not fall into the confusion of mistaking normal aloneness, which is intended to draw us to God.

You must fill your time with activities that are God oriented, as mentioned above, spending time with him, so that he can tell you about yourself, and himself.

Women and men, who live by themselves and who are well adjusted are simply those who have recognized this secret place as His, and have allowed Him to enter and take possession of what is his rightful place.

The maladjusted Christian will experience this aloneness, and not be aware of what it is, will leap to the wrong conclusions, and begin to scream that they are lonely.

No, recognize this is just God's way of telling you that he wants to hear your voice, and feel your embrace.

Loneliness is different from aloneness (pp. 148-149, Woman to Woman). This aloneness is a warning light or signal that it is time for God and you to fellowship in prayer, conversation and meditation on his 'Standard Operating Procedures' (Bible) to fill that moment in your life with what should be there to bring you closer to your expected end.

An old cliche says, if it don't fit, don't (what – force it)? Please put what fits in that place, at that particular moment, rather than an imperfect human being. It has been this way since the fall of Adam, mentioned in Chapter One of this book, and in Genesis. Originally, God made us for his glory, and we were the praise of his handiwork, the coming of His son Emmanuel and his resurrection replaced what had been stolen.

You see man had touched the glory, and clearly the word of God, says that MAN, should not touch the glory, because all glory, all honor, and all power belong to him. In Genesis 3:2-3 "And the woman said...God has said "You shall not eat it, nor shall you touch it, lest you die."(NKJV)

Jesus said, he would pour himself out, in Acts 2:17, and what is himself. It is the sufficiency of God, the blood and water that gives the life to us into the empty recesses left by the great fall! Get in position to be poured into, what had been lost is now found!!!

O' taste and see that the Lord, he is good. (Psalms 34:8)

Whether you are divorced, widowed, or never married. He is the same who is with us when we are in the valley, on the mountain-top, by the stream, crossing the river, or about to faint. He is waiting for you at the end of this corner, located at 0000 Yourself Street. In other words at the end of yourself. So, go quickly, and meet him, he is waiting! Don't make the wrong turn, there are no turns, or detours, but he is straight ahead.

I have outlined some doors that the enemy will use to distract you, and lure you with if you let him below. Know the plots of the enemy, and by all means don't open that door. If you have and are already there, you can walk out and close the door behind you. Plead the blood of Jesus over the door, and commit to forgetting what is behind and press ahead.

E- Don't Open that Door

Fornication:
Sex between unmarried persons. Acts 15: 19-20, I Corinthians 7:2, Hebrews 13:4

Adultery:
 Sex between two persons, one of which is married or both are married, but not to each other. Matthew 15:18-20, Hebrews 13:4

Immorality:
Unchecked, destructive passion. II Samuel 13:1-20, Romans 7:8, Colossians 3: 4-5, I Thessalonians 4:3-5

Let us put away childish behavior, and go in search of whom your soul loveth. Read I Corinthians 13:11 & Song of Solomon 3:1-3.

REMEMBER:
"The female is the lock, and the male is the key. Apart from each other they don't fulfill the purpose of which they were designed. That is to secure those things, which are God given to them as a family ordained by God. A single woman has God as her key, and a single man has God as his lock. All things exist in Him!"

CHAPTER 12

A CHRISTIAN PARENTS'
SEXUALITY & PARENTING

12- A Christian Parents' Sexuality & Parenting

A – Christ Controlled

It is paramount that a parent train their child(ren) creatively with God's help, and not damage their personality. A child will become what the mother and father influences him or her to become. The mother teaches as her husband teaches her, and he teaches as God teaches him, and both teach as God leads them. They are taught how to love themselves and others, by their parents' examples and teachings.

B- Don't Hinder the Children

The manner in which we conduct ourselves before our children when we are unmarried is critical to their perception and understanding of the value that God places on intimacy. What they see you do is what they will replicate in their relationship choices. You may tell them not to do this or that, but if you are doing this or that; what more should they be expected to do. Hindering them in this area sets them up for early pregnancy, emotional baggage and sexually transmitted diseases. They will be ill prepared to enter into lasting relationships or see commitment as necessary.

Jesus said " it is beter to have a millstone tied about your neck than to hinder the little ones.

C- Shacking Up and Dating

One-hearted parents should never consider common law marriage. Carrying on, and heavy petting before God or your child(ren) should not even be an issue. The men should be just as conservative in this area, because they are the high priest in this area. The Bible declares that we are to train up a child in the way he should go.

If you desire to date and are dating, get to know that person away from your child, better before you introduce them to your children. Never bring them to your home on first, second or third dates. Meet on neutral ground without your child(ren). Preferably with a chaperone. Especially if you are highly sensitive sexually. We are to be chaste and suitable for the mate God ordained.

Try to double date on your first date. Then as the Holy Spirit leads you go on dates, and always be up front with your date about your children.

Three areas that must be healed:
1) A broken heart
2) A crushed spirit, and
3) A painful soul.

This is why I do not recommend dating. Especially until you have sufficiently healed these areas of your being. A broken heart needs to be mended by the word of Luke 4:18. Because your spirit has been crushed and a death has taken place. Proverbs 15:13, Proverbs 17:22 tells us that it dries up the bones, and sinew. The bones are the factory for blood, life is in that blood. Proverbs 18:14, speaks of depression as a result of being rejected. But there is a Balm in Gilead, even Psalms 34:17-19, says the Lord delivers. When we feel unlovely, and distanced, God is never nearer to us.

So your relationship failed, but God never does, and you are not a failure. A hurting person will only draw more hurting people to themselves. And hurting people, hurt other people. They draw wounded vagabonds, leaches, and bats into their environment. Don't smile on the outside in an attempt to camouflage your pain. Surround yourself with the word of God, and healed emotional people. The Bible says that we who are strong are to bear the infirmities of the weak. Until they can bear themselves up.

Take control over your life, nurse it back, lay it out before the sun "SON" so that your life can be refreshed back to wholeness and health. If you were or/are co-dependent in relationships, now is the time to get out of that and into dependency on God. There is nothing too hard for God. Submit to his healing process, learn how to draw boundary lines, destroy soul ties, and take root in God's restoring soil of salvation.

Endnotes

M A T E R I A L S
Bibles: King James Version

Books:
Myles Munroe, copyright 1991
Single, Married, Separated & Life After Divorce
Bahamas Faith Ministries Published by Vincom, Inc.
P.O. Box 702400
Tulsa, OK 74170
Reprint Permission Granted by Vincom, Inc.

Eugenia Price
Woman to Woman, copyright 1959
Zondervan Books
Zondervan Publishing House
Grand Rapids, MI 49506
Used by Permission of Zondervan Publishing House

Derek and Ruth Prince
God Is A Matchmaker, 1986
Chosen Books a Division of Baker Book House
P.O. Box 6287
Grand Rapids, MI 49516-6287
Used by Permission of Baker Book House

Spiros Zodhiates
The Complete Word Study – New Testament
Chattanooga, TN 37422
AMG Publishers, 1991
6815 Shallowford Rd.
Box 22000
Reprint Permission Granted by AMG Publishers

Other Volumes in the One Heart Series by Patricia E. Adams

VOLUME 1
With Oneness of Heart
ISBN 0-9700976-0-3
Formats: Paper, Audio, E-Book & Digital, Kindle
 Book: Disciple's Guide
Audio: Disciple's Overview

VOLUME 2
Book: Journeying to the Road Called Oneness
ISBN 0-9700976-1-1
Formats: Paper, Audio, E-Book & Digital, Kindle
 Book: Disciple's Guide
Audio: Disciple's Overview

VOLUME 3
Detouring off the Road of Oneness
ISBN 0-9700976-2-X
Formats: Paper, Audio, E-Book & Digital, Kindle
Book: Disciple's Guide
Audio: Disciple's Overview

VOLUME 4
I and My Father Are One
ISBN 0-9700976-3-8
Formats: Paper, Audio, E-Book & Digital, Kindle
 Book: Disciple's Guide
Audio: Disciple's Overview

VOLUME 5
52 Week Devotional & Journal Study/Application
ISBN 09700976-7-0
Formats: Paperback

Website: www.oneheartseries.com
Affiliate Program: www.oneheartseriesaffiliates.com
Radio Network: www.oneheartsoundmedianetwork.com
Email: author@oneheartseries.com